JESUS
THE CHRIST

**Roman Bridge over the Tagus River
at Alcántara, Spain**

Roman Encampment

Tiberius

Roman Soldiers

Augustus

The Temple in Jerusalem

THE BIBLE
AND
ITS STORY

1

THE CREATION

2

THE PATRIARCHS
AND MOSES

3

IN THE PROMISED LAND

4

KINGS AND PROPHETS

5

EXILE AND RETURN

6

JESUS THE CHRIST

7

THE LORD'S FOLLOWERS

Planned and produced by
Jaca Book — Le Centurion
from the ideas of
Charles Ehlinger, Hervé Lauriot Prévost,
Pierre Talec, and the editorial committee
of Jaca Book

A chapter outline for this volume
is printed on the last two pages
of the volume.

JESUS THE CHRIST

THE BIBLE AND ITS STORY

Text by Enrico Galbiati, Elio Guerriero, Antonio Sicari
Translation by Kenneth D. Whitehead
Illustrations by Antonio Molino

 Winston Press 430 Oak Grove   Minneapolis, Minnesota 55403

Published in Italy under the title
Gesù il Cristo
Copyright © 1983 Jaca Book—Le Centurion

**Licensed publisher and distributor
of the English-language edition:**
Winston Press, Inc.
430 Oak Grove
Minneapolis, Minnesota 55403
United States of America

Agents:
Canada—
LeDroit/Novalis-Select
135 Nelson Street
Ottawa, Ontario
Canada K1N 7R4

Australia, New Zealand, New Guinea, Fiji Islands—
Dove Communications, Pty. Ltd.
Suite 1, 60-64 Railway Road
Blackburn, Victoria 3130
Australia

Winston Scriptural Consultant:
Catherine Litecky, CSJ
Department of Theology
College of St. Catherine
St. Paul, Minnesota

Winston Staff:
Hermann Weinlick—editorial
Reg Sandland, Kathe Wilcoxon—design

Jaca Book—Le Centurion Editorial Committee:
François Brossier, Maretta Campi, Charles Ehlinger,
Enrico Galbiati, Elio Guerriero, Pierre Talec

General Coordination: Caterina Longanesi
Color selection: Carlo Scotti, Milan, Italy
Printing: Gorenjski tisk, Kranj, Yugoslavia

Library of Congress Catalog Card Number: 83-50472
ISBN: 0-86683-196-7

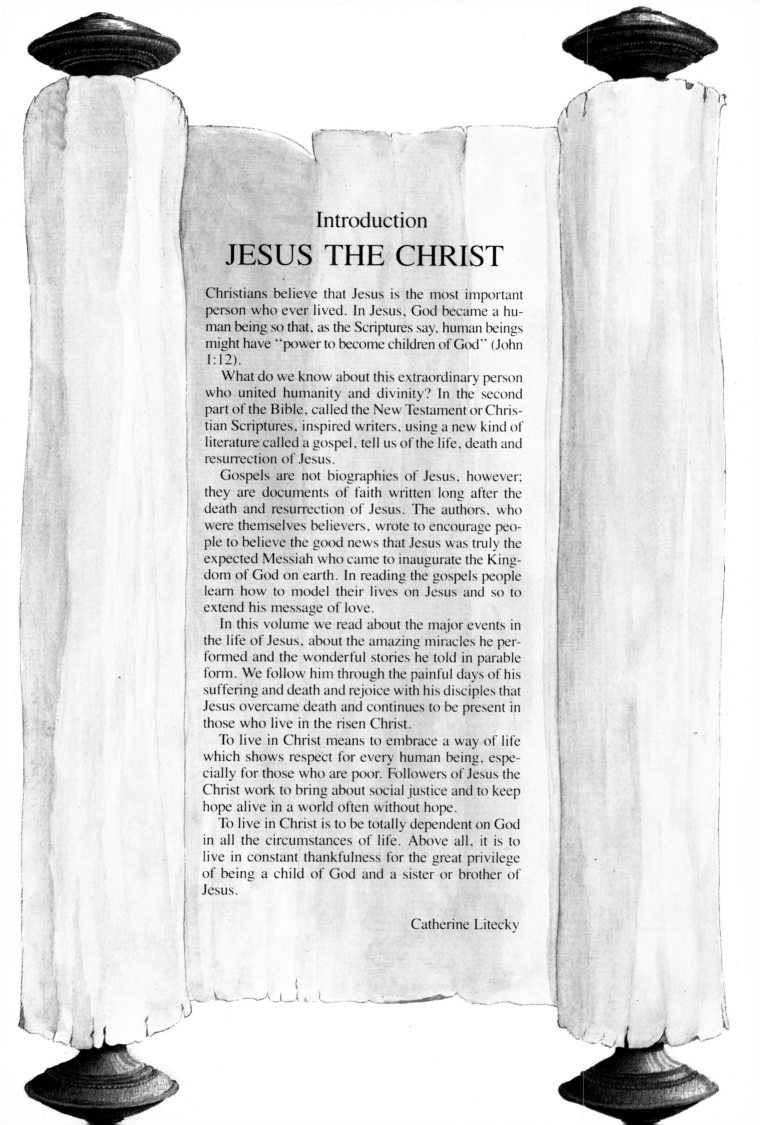

Introduction
JESUS THE CHRIST

Christians believe that Jesus is the most important person who ever lived. In Jesus, God became a human being so that, as the Scriptures say, human beings might have "power to become children of God" (John 1:12).

What do we know about this extraordinary person who united humanity and divinity? In the second part of the Bible, called the New Testament or Christian Scriptures, inspired writers, using a new kind of literature called a gospel, tell us of the life, death and resurrection of Jesus.

Gospels are not biographies of Jesus, however; they are documents of faith written long after the death and resurrection of Jesus. The authors, who were themselves believers, wrote to encourage people to believe the good news that Jesus was truly the expected Messiah who came to inaugurate the Kingdom of God on earth. In reading the gospels people learn how to model their lives on Jesus and so to extend his message of love.

In this volume we read about the major events in the life of Jesus, about the amazing miracles he performed and the wonderful stories he told in parable form. We follow him through the painful days of his suffering and death and rejoice with his disciples that Jesus overcame death and continues to be present in those who live in the risen Christ.

To live in Christ means to embrace a way of life which shows respect for every human being, especially for those who are poor. Followers of Jesus the Christ work to bring about social justice and to keep hope alive in a world often without hope.

To live in Christ is to be totally dependent on God in all the circumstances of life. Above all, it is to live in constant thankfulness for the great privilege of being a child of God and a sister or brother of Jesus.

Catherine Litecky

1 When Jesus died, about A.D. 30,
his disciples were very sad
and discouraged.
Then they discovered
that Jesus had been raised
from the dead.
After that they wanted
to tell the whole world
about Jesus.

A most extraordinary man, a prophet named Jesus, attracted attention in Galilee and Judea, arousing the enthusiasm of the crowds and the hatred of some of the authorities. Many witnesses told amazing stories about him; he performed actual miracles, greater in number and more wonderful than those of the ancient prophets themselves. Some people believed he was the Messiah who, according to the ancient prophecies, would restore the kingdom of Israel.

However, popular enthusiasm soon subsided, and disappointment set in. This Jesus who possessed so many marvelous powers could have led an armed revolt against the Romans; but instead he spoke only of love and pardon. The kingdom of God which he preached and promised apparently had little to do with the Jewish desire for a free nation.

Eventually Jesus' enemies succeeded in having him condemned to death by the Roman governor, Pontius Pilate. He was nailed to a cross between two thieves. All reason for hope in Jesus seemed to die with him.

But then new and even more extraordinary things began to happen. His disciples found that the tomb where he had been buried was empty. They encountered him as one who had risen; they knew him as they had known him before his crucifixion.

Then his closest disciples became preachers and miracle workers, as Jesus himself had been. They persuaded large numbers of people that Jesus in fact had been the Messiah; that he had been crucified and had risen from the dead; that he was the Son of God. Everyone was to receive baptism in his name, to gather together to celebrate a sacred meal as he had celebrated it before his crucifixion, and to live a life of goodness and love for one another.

Those who responded called themselves by the name of Jesus' original followers, "the disciples." Very soon communities of these disciples could be found in the important centers of Judea, from Jerusalem all the way to Lydda, Jaffa, and Caesarea, where the Roman governor resided. They were found as far away as Antioch, the capital of Syria, where numerous pagans had embraced the new faith in Jesus Christ. It was in Antioch that the disciples were called "Christians" for the first time.

The new Christians had an intense desire to know more about Jesus, whom they had seen only occasionally or not at all. So they gathered around those very first disciples, the apostles, to hear them repeat incidents from Jesus' life and the very words Jesus had spoken in his teaching. The apostles, who had been Jesus' students, had learned the words of his teachings by heart, and they remembered the events of his life.

Now they saw his life and teachings in a new light, in the light of his resurrection from the dead. They also looked again at the ancient Jewish prophecies and compared them with the life of Jesus; they found in Scripture further evidence that Jesus was the Messiah and the Son of God.

IMAGO LEONIS

IMAGO HOMINIS

2. For a few decades the good news,
the gospel, about Jesus
was passed on by word of mouth.
Between A.D. 65 and 100,
sayings of Jesus
and stories about his life
were preserved in the four books
we call gospels:
Matthew, Mark, Luke, and John.

For several decades the apostles and their disciples were content to pass on by word of mouth the traditions about the life and teachings of Jesus to inspire faith and instruct the new communities of Christians. This preaching of the apostles was given a Greek name *evangelion,* which means "good news." Our English word "gospel" also means "good news." Jesus himself had given the name "good news" to his own message—a message about the love of the God who offered salvation to all people and invited them into the kingdom.

After some years of teaching only by memory, some Christian preachers began to prepare written notes to aid their preaching. And so there came into existence collections of the sayings and parables of Jesus, episodes in his life, and stories of his passion, or suffering. Because these had been told many, many times over, they had assumed rather fixed forms.

At this point, the "evangelists" came upon the scene. They were the persons who wrote down not merely notes but entire books that were themselves given the name of "gospels." The gospel, the good news about Jesus, was one single story, though it was written down by several different writers.

The first of these gospels in our Bibles is written by a man named Matthew. Matthew had been

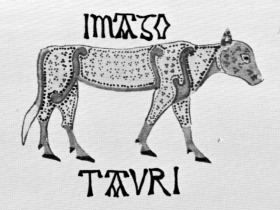

IMAGO TAVRI

IMAGO AQVILE

a "publican," or tax collector in the little town of Capernaum. After Jesus called him to be a disciple, he left everything immediately to follow Jesus. It is thought that he wrote his gospel for the benefit of Jews who had become Christian. He wrote it in Aramaic, the language of the Jews, and often quoted the Old Testament. He emphasized the truth of Jesus' sayings over the erroneous traditions of the Pharisees. Some Pharisees were very influential in the Christian communities composed of former Jews. Matthew's work was translated into Greek and reworked by an unknown author, perhaps around A.D. 70 or 80. It is this reworked version that we possess and call the Gospel of Matthew.

According to early church tradition, the author of the second gospel is Mark; Mark calls his book "the Good News about Jesus Christ, the Son of God" (Mark 1:1 TEV). John Mark was born in Jerusalem of a Greek-speaking family that had come originally from Cyprus. He was not an apostle, although when he was very young he may have known Jesus. He was a follower and helper of Paul, and then of Peter. He wrote his gospel in Rome around A.D. 70 for the benefit of those Christians who had been Gentiles. Because the original version of Matthew has not come down to us, many scholars believe that Mark produced the first written gospel.

The third evangelist was called Luke. He was probably born in Antioch and a Gentile convert. Some think that he was a physician. He wrote with great skill and sensitivity. He probably wrote down his gospel before A.D. 80. Luke also wrote the Acts of the Apostles, about the early days of the church, as a sequel to his gospel.

The fourth evangelist was John. He wrote his very original gospel at Ephesus, perhaps as late as A.D. 100. His gospel contains his own reflections on the divinity of Jesus.

Four different symbols have traditionally been applied to the evangelists: a *man* for Matthew (because he began with the human genealogy of Jesus); a *lion* for Mark (because he began with the preaching of John the Baptist in the wilderness); a *calf* for Luke (because he began with the story of Zechariah in the Temple where calves and lambs were sacrificed); an *eagle* for John (because in his contemplation of the divinity of Jesus he soared heavenward like an eagle). These symbols were derived from "the four living creatures" (Revelation 4:6) seated around the throne of God, as described in the Book of Revelation (Apocalypse).

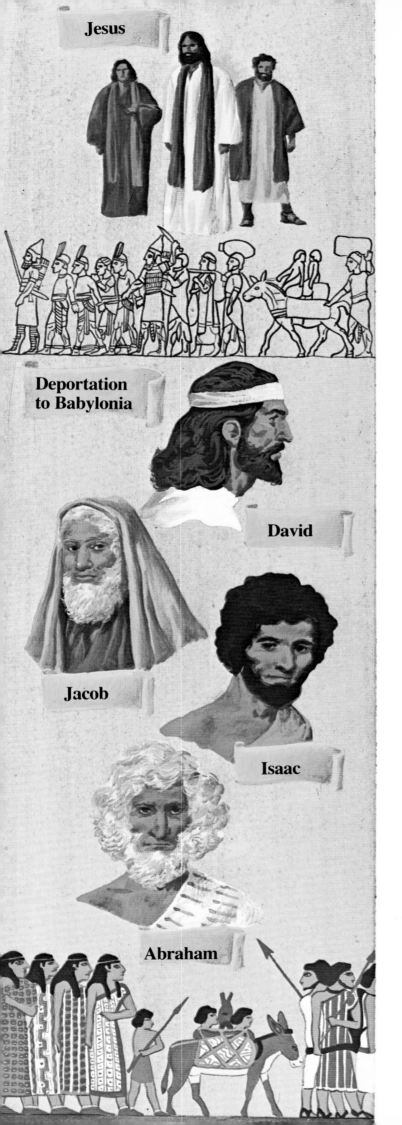

Jesus

Deportation to Babylonia

David

Jacob

Isaac

Abraham

3
Matthew and Luke list
the ancestors of Jesus.
Matthew emphasizes Jesus'
relationship to King David.
Luke stresses how Jesus
is related to all people.

Matthew, in his first chapter, and Luke, in his third chapter, each gave a genealogy for Jesus, a list of his ancestors. As a human being, born of Mary, Jesus was a descendant of famous persons who had looked to a future salvation that had been promised, and who had handed down to their descendants the hopes of a Messiah to come. The evangelists wanted to demonstrate that in Jesus these hopes had been fulfilled.

However, the genealogy supplied by Matthew does not coincide exactly with the one supplied by Luke. Matthew wrote for the Jews, the Chosen People, who were proud of being Abraham's descendants. So Matthew began his genealogy with Abraham: "The book of the genealogy of Jesus Christ, the son of David, the son of Abraham. Abraham was the father of Isaac, and Isaac the father of Jacob" (Matthew 1:1-2).

With Abraham a new era in the history of salvation had begun. With the election of Abraham, God had begun to prepare the way for the future Messiah; God had told Abraham: "I will make of you a great nation . . . and by you all the families of the earth shall bless themselves" (Genesis 12:2,3). Jesus was the one who, descended from Abraham, provided the fulfillment of that blessing.

David had been the "first" Messiah, that is, the king consecrated by means of a sacred anointing. Through the prophet Nathan, God had promised David that one of his descendants would rule

over an eternal kingdom (2 Samuel 7:13). This prophecy, expanded and made clearer by Isaiah and other prophets, had created among the Jews the expectation of a future Messiah, a descendant of David. The followers of Jesus believed that he was this Messiah-King; in him the prophecy was fulfilled. Matthew divided his genealogy into three periods of fourteen generations each: from Abraham to David, from David to the deportation to Babylon, from the deportation to Babylon down to Jesus. In the second part of this genealogy, the kings of Judah were listed to emphasize the hereditary line of David.

While Matthew started with Abraham and moved to Jesus, Luke followed the line from Jesus back to Abraham, the founder of the Jewish race; and then on back to Adam, the beginning of the entire human race. In this way, Luke declared that Jesus belonged to the whole human family and affirmed his solidarity with all persons of whatever race. The salvation brought by Jesus was universal; it was for all.

The names used by Luke in his genealogy were taken from chapters five and eleven of the Book of Genesis, where the patriarchs from Adam to Noah and from Noah to Abraham are listed. However, the names were not what most interested the evangelist. The most important message was that Jesus had come with the task of saving all.

4 Luke and Matthew are
the only gospels with stories
of the birth of Jesus.
Luke tells how Mary learns
that she is to be
the mother of Jesus.

Matthew and Luke are the only two evangelists who have provided us with any information about the birth of Jesus and his first few years. Luke tells first about the birth of John, who would later be called John the Baptist. John's parents, Zechariah and Elizabeth, had grown old without having children. Zechariah was a priest; one day as he entered the sanctuary to burn incense, he saw an angel of the Lord. The angel announced that Elizabeth would bear a son who would carry out a very important mission in Israel. Dazzled by this revelation, Zechariah hesitated a moment. How could it be? He and Elizabeth were already too old. Because his hesitation showed a lack of faith, Zechariah became mute until the birth of the child.

Some six months later an angel appeared to a relative of hers, a young woman named Mary. She was engaged to Joseph, who lived in the town of Nazareth. The angel declared, "Hail, O favored one, the Lord is with you!" (Luke 1:28). Mary was greatly upset by these words and did not know what they meant.

The angel said to her, "Don't be afraid, Mary; God has been gracious to you. You will become pregnant and give birth to a son, and you will name him Jesus." Mary said to the angel, "I am a virgin. How, then, can this be?"

The angel answered, "The Holy Spirit will come on you, and God's power will rest upon you. For this reason the holy child will be called the Son of God."

"I am the Lord's servant," said Mary; "may it happen to me as you have said." And the angel left her.   (Luke 1:30-31,34-35,38 TEV)

Mary went to visit her relative Elizabeth, who also awaited an unusual birth. This meeting resulted in Mary's hymn of praise to God, in which she glorified God as the enemy of the proud and the defender of the lowly.

"My soul magnifies the Lord,
and my spirit rejoices in God my Savior,
for he has regarded the low estate of his
    handmaiden.
For behold, henceforth all generations will
    call me blessed;
for he who is mighty has done great things
    for me,
and holy is his name.
And his mercy is on those who fear him
from generation to generation.
He has shown strength with his arm,
he has scattered the proud in the imagination
    of their hearts,
he has put down the mighty from their
    thrones,
and exalted those of low degree;
he has filled the hungry with good things,
and the rich he has sent empty away.
He has helped his servant Israel,
in remembrance of his mercy,
as he spoke to our fathers,
to Abraham and to his posterity for ever."
                                    (Luke 1:46-55)

The members of the community turned to the boy's father, who was still mute. Zechariah wrote on a tablet, "His name is John" (Luke 1:63 TEV). At this point Zechariah was able to speak again. He immediately began to praise God for all that God had done and for the gift of a son.

Mary stayed three months with Elizabeth. Then Elizabeth gave birth to a son. According to the established custom, members of the community called upon Elizabeth eight days after the birth to circumcize the child and initiate him into the community. They all thought the boy should be named Zechariah after his father, but Elizabeth refused. "No! His name is to be John" (Luke 1:60 TEV).

5 Luke tells the story
of the birth of Jesus
in Bethlehem of Judea.
Some shepherds
and two older persons,
Simeon and Anna,
learned that Jesus
was the Messiah.

Luke was the evangelist who reflected most on the significance of human events. The events of history are arranged by God to realize God's designs for human salvation. At the time of Jesus' birth Palestine was under the domination of Rome, while the Roman Empire was ruled by the emperor Augustus.

Augustus ordered that a census be taken in Palestine as he had done in other provinces. Each family had to appear before the Roman authorities to provide the necessary information about itself. This was no particular problem for those who still lived in the towns where their families had lived for generations, but it was a burden for those who lived elsewhere. This was the case for Joseph, Mary's husband. Because Joseph was a descendant of David, he had to go from his home in Nazareth in Galilee to Bethlehem in Judea, where David had lived.

This was a difficult journey of around ninety miles; it was particularly difficult because Mary was pregnant and about to give birth.

In fact Mary did give birth to a son while they were in Bethlehem. She wrapped up the child and laid him in a manger, a feed trough for animals. Mary and Joseph were poor people, and they had not been able to obtain any lodging at the town's inn.

Not far from the stable where the child was born that night, there were bands of shepherds taking care of their flocks. Suddenly they saw a great light. An angel of the lord appeared to them.

But the angel said to them, "Don't be afraid! I am here with good news for you, which will bring great joy to all the people. This very day

in David's town your Savior was born—Christ the Lord! And this is what will prove it to you: you will find a baby wrapped in cloths and lying in a manger."

Suddenly a great army of heaven's angels appeared with the angel, singing praises to God:

"Glory to God in the highest
heaven,
and peace on earth to those
with whom he is pleased!"

(Luke 2:10-14 TEV)

It all happened in a moment. When the vision disappeared, the shepherds hurried to follow the angel's directions. They found the baby lying in the manger. Then they returned to their flocks, glorifying and praising God.

According to the prescriptions of the Law of Moses, the newborn child had to be consecrated to the Lord on the eighth day through the rite of circumcision, a ritual that commemorated the Covenant of God with his people. On that occasion, the child was given the name of Jesus, as the angel had told Mary at the time of the annunciation.

But the religious requirements connected with the birth of a baby were not yet completed. After forty days, Joseph, Mary, and Jesus traveled the few miles from Bethlehem to Jerusalem and visited the Temple to present Jesus to the Lord.

Mary and Joseph were offering a sacrifice in the Temple when an old man approached. He was Simeon, a pious Jew who was spending his last days in the Temple, awaiting the coming of the Messiah. When he saw the child Jesus, Simeon was inspired by the Holy Spirit to recognize in him the Messiah of Israel.

Another person joined the group, an old prophetess named Anna, who also spent her time in the Temple awaiting the coming of the Messiah. She too was inspired by the Holy Spirit and praised God for having sent the liberator of Israel.

So, according to Luke's account, the birth of Jesus was announced at the time to all the people of Israel, represented by the shepherds, by a just man, and by a prophetess. But the first witnesses of this great event were humble shepherds whose names have not even been handed down to us. The humble birth of Jesus anticipated Jesus' later preaching in support of the poor and humble.

6 Matthew tells of wise men
from an eastern country
who came to worship young Jesus.
King Herod was afraid that
the baby would take away
his power.
So he killed many babies
while trying to kill Jesus.

Matthew's gospel agrees with Luke's concerning fundamental facts about Jesus' birth: Mary found herself pregnant by the Holy Spirit; Jesus had no human father (his conception took place before she went to live with Joseph); Jesus was born in Bethlehem, the city of David, in the last years of Herod the Great's reign.

Matthew added to this basic account the appearance of the angel to Joseph to explain to him the supernatural origin of Mary's child. Then, as if he knew nothing of the relationship between the births of Jesus and John the Baptist, the revelation given to the shepherds, or the presentation of Jesus in the Temple, Matthew moved to a later period in the life of the infant Jesus. He told the story of the magi, or wise men, from the east who came to Jerusalem inquiring, "Where is he who has been born king of the Jews?" (Matthew 2:2).

There may have been three of these wise men; Matthew did not say. They were probably not "kings," or Matthew would have said so. As "magi," or "magicians," they probably were Persians who studied the stars. They had taken note of an extraordinary star or constellation, and concluded from it that the expected Messiah of the Jews finally had been born. So they had come to Jerusalem, assuming that the Messiah-King was to be found in the capital.

At that time the king of Judea was Herod the Great; he had reigned for more than thirty years and was now old. Fearful for his throne, he had already condemned to death two of his own sons, and before he died he would have another one killed.

Herod had heard that the wise men wanted to find Jesus and worship him. This news upset him, but he concealed his jealous worries. He asked his scribes and priests where this Messiah was to be born; they told him that according to Micah's prophecy he was to be born in Bethlehem. Herod then secretly called in the wise men and asked them when the star had appeared; he recommended that they go to Bethlehem to search for the newborn Messiah: "Go and search diligently for the child, and when you have found him, bring me word, that I too may come and worship him" (Matthew 2:8).

The magi left Herod and headed towards Bethlehem, less than six miles away. It was almost night, and the star they had seen in the east served as their guide. They followed it until they came to the house where Jesus was lying with his mother Mary. There the wise men fell down and worshiped the child. From their baggage they took out gold, frankincense, and myrrh, characteristic products of their country, as gifts.

Perhaps without knowing it, they offered gifts that symbolized the mysterious personality of the child: gold, for a king; frankincense, for God; and myrrh, a substance used in burial, for one who would die on the cross for the love of humanity.

That night the magi were warned in a vision not to return to see Herod. Joseph also was warned in a vision to flee to Egypt with the mother and child.

Herod was tormented constantly by jealousy and by suspicion of plots against him. When the magi did not return to tell him what they had found, he initiated efforts to put Jesus to death. Since he could not identify a particular baby among all those in Bethlehem, he ordered his soldiers to kill all the boys there up to two years old. That way he felt sure of including the Messiah in the slaughter.

By then, however, Jesus was already on the way to Egypt. He would not be brought back to Israel until after Herod's death. Joseph might have wanted to return to Bethlehem, but Archelaus, who was then ruling, was even more cruel than his father Herod had been. So Joseph decided to return to his old home in Galilee. The young Herod Antipas ruled peacefully in Galilee, concerned only with his own amusements.

7 The gospels say very little
about the boyhood of Jesus,
except for one story.
When Jesus was twelve,
his family went to Jerusalem.
His parents became worried
when they couldn't find Jesus.
They finally found him
in the Temple.
He had stayed there
to talk with teachers.

Jesus was still very small when the family returned from Egypt and settled in the village of Nazareth. Joseph worked as a carpenter, constructing items such as plows, yokes for oxen, doors, and ceiling beams for the larger houses.

The gospels tell us almost nothing about the boyhood of Jesus, certainly nothing marvelous or out of the ordinary; Luke recorded only that Jesus grew in wisdom, stature, and grace. Apparently he grew up as a boy remarkable only for an intelligence beyond his years. Mary and Joseph treated him as any other boy; they put him to work at various tasks and expected obedience from him.

The evangelists record only one episode that disturbed the family's tranquility. Jewish Law prescribed three annual pilgrimages to Jerusalem for those who lived within a day's journey of the city: on the feasts of the Passover, Pentecost, and the Booths. For people who lived more than a day's journey away, these pilgrimages were not required.

Nazareth was three or four days' journey from Jerusalem. However, Joseph, like many religious

Jews, tried to get to Jerusalem at least for the Passover. On this important Jewish feast, the Passover lamb was supposed to be sacrificed in the Temple and then eaten in Jerusalem. This feast commemorated Israel's last night of bondage in Egypt, when the blood of a sacrificial lamb marked Hebrew houses and the angel of death "passed over" them.

Because of his youth, Jesus did not have to make these pilgrimages, but he apparently was used to going with Joseph and Mary. The feast of the Passover lasted seven days, although after the third day many pilgrims began gathering their baggage and leaving the holy city.

Joseph and Mary joined one of the caravans and began the return journey to Nazareth. They lost sight of Jesus, but they assumed he was among the other boys belonging to the caravan, or with relatives or friends. When evening came and the caravan halted for the night, Jesus was nowhere to be found.

Greatly worried, Mary and Joseph feared that some misfortune had befallen Jesus. At the first light of dawn they returned hastily to Jerusalem. They searched everywhere in the city for Jesus and after three days they finally found him in the Temple. In a portico, in one of the rooms open to the public, the boy sat with a group of teachers of the Law, experts in Scripture. He asked and answered questions with such intelligence and knowledge that all who heard him were amazed.

Mary asked Jesus in a voice filled with anxiety, "Son, why have you treated us so? Behold, your father and I have been looking for you anxiously" (Luke 2:48).

The answer Jesus gave was a very mysterious one: "How is it that you sought me? Did you not know that I must be in my Father's house?" (Luke 2:49).

Jesus placed his Father in heaven ahead even of Mary and Joseph. Fulfilling the will of God would sometimes mean sacrificing the affections of those most dear to him. However, Jesus then returned to Nazareth with his parents, and, as he grew up, was respectful and obedient toward them.

8 During the public life of Jesus, around A.D. 30, Palestine was part of the Roman Empire. Galilee, in northern Palestine, was ruled by Herod Antipas. Most of Palestine was under a Roman governor named Pontius Pilate.

The public life of Jesus—the period from the time he began to preach until his death on the cross—unfolded during the years A.D. 28-30.

The emperor Tiberius had ruled the Roman Empire since the year A.D. 14. The empire had not yet quite grown to its maximum size. However, it already included Italy, the Iberian peninsula (modern Spain and Portugal), Gaul (modern France), Dalmatia (modern Yugoslavia), and Greece. Its northern borders in Europe were along the Rhine and the Danube rivers. German and other barbarian tribes inhabited the land beyond these borders. Rome controlled the African coast from Numidia (modern Algeria) to Egypt. In the east the empire controlled Asia Minor (modern Turkey) and Syria all the way to the Euphrates River; this territory included the vassal kingdoms of Cappadocia, Armenia, and the provinces in Palestine governed by the successors of Herod.

Herod had obtained from the Romans a kingdom called Judea, which included all of Palestine and some territories next to it. At Herod's death in 4 B.C., this kingdom was divided among his sons. Jesus was already born by this time. (Strange as it may seem, Jesus was born several years "before Christ." This is because the B.C. and A.D. numbering systems came into use long after Jesus lived. A.D. comes from the Latin words *anno domini*, which mean "in the year of our Lord.")

The emperor Caesar Augustus, however, did not allow Herod's successors to bear the title of king. The eldest son Archelaus governed *Judea* and *Samaria* with the title of "ethnarch," or "ruler of the nation." Because of his great cruelty, he was deposed by the emperor in A.D. 6, after ruling nine years and sent into exile. The territories he had governed then came under direct Roman control. They were dependent upon the province of Syria but were ruled directly by a Roman governor who had the title of "prefect" or "procurator." This official resided in Caesarea but maintained a strong military garrison in Jerusa-lem, where he moved with a military escort during the great feasts to control the crowds and prevent disorders or rebellions. Thus it was that during the decisive week of Jesus' life the Roman procurator Pontius Pilate was in Jerusalem. Without his cooperation, the enemies of Jesus would not have been able to execute the death sentence on him.

The younger son of Herod was Herod Antipas. He ruled *Galilee* (the northernmost part of Palestine) and a territory east of the Jordan river called *Perea*. Herod Antipas also did not bear the title king, but rather "tetrarch," or "ruler of the fourth part." This son of Herod I built the city of Tiberias, on the Sea of Galilee, in honor of the Roman emperor Tiberius.

A grandson of Herod I named Philip also bore the title of tetrarch and ruled over territories northeast of the Sea of Galilee that included modern Golan and Hauran. Philip enlarged the town of Paneas, near one of the sources of the Jordan, and gave it the name of Caesarea in honor of the emperor. This was the Caesarea Philippi mentioned in the gospels. Herod's successors were not given the free cities of the *Decapolis* ("ten cities") to rule; these cities, governed according to their own laws, were annexed to the province of Syria. Nearly all of them were located east of the Jordan. They were inhabited mostly by Gentiles and not by Jews. The principal cities were Gadara and Gerasa.

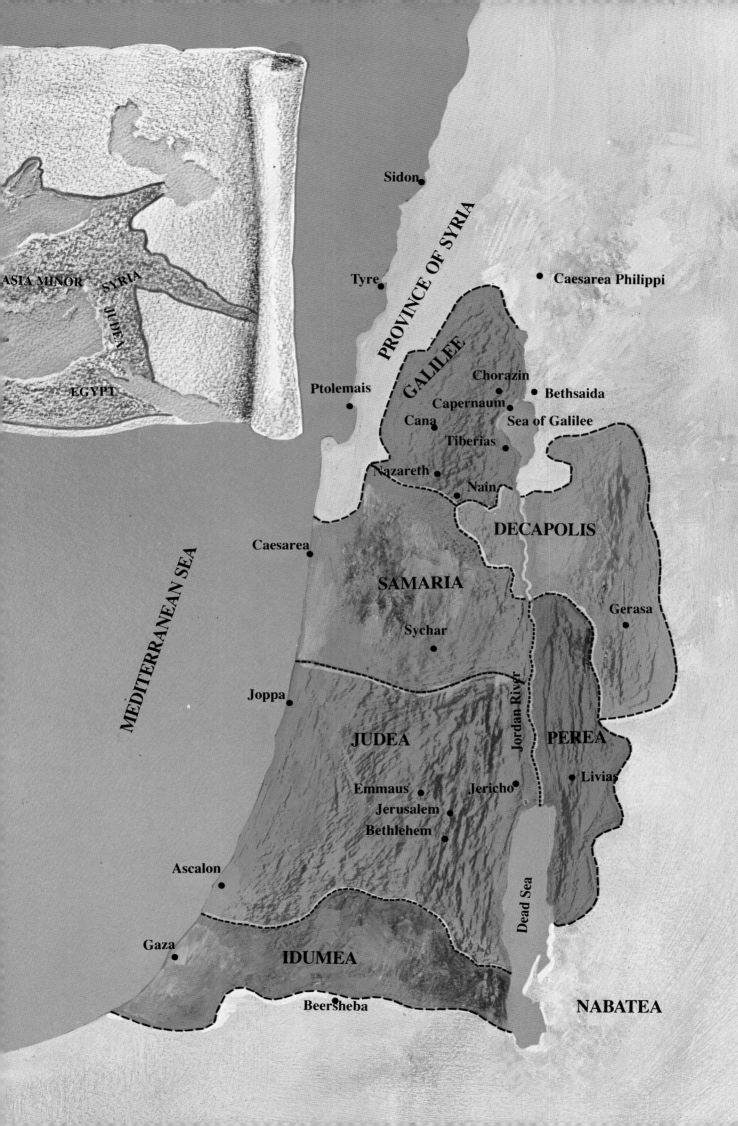

Sidon

PROVINCE OF SYRIA

Tyre

Caesarea Philippi

GALILEE

Ptolemais

Chorazin

Capernaum

Bethsaida

Cana

Sea of Galilee

Tiberias

Nazareth

Nain

DECAPOLIS

Caesarea

SAMARIA

Sychar

Gerasa

MEDITERRANEAN SEA

Joppa

Jordan River

JUDEA

PEREA

Emmaus

Jericho

Livias

Jerusalem

Bethlehem

Dead Sea

Ascalon

Gaza

IDUMEA

Beersheba

NABATEA

ASIA MINOR

SYRIA

JUDEA

EGYPT

9 In the time of Jesus various groups or parties existed among the Jews: Sadducees, Pharisees, zealots, Essenes. Priests, scribes, and rabbis studied and passed on Jewish religious traditions.

There was a compact majority of Jews living in both Judea and Galilee. However, between these two territories lay Samaria, the country inhabited by the Samaritans. The Samaritans were of mixed origin racially. Their religion resembled the religion practiced by the Jews; they too used the first five books of the Bible, the Pentateuch. However, most Jews thought that the Samaritans had been defiled by foreign elements and were no better than Gentiles.

Among the Jews themselves there were strong differences in social conditions and in outlook and ideas. The priests serving in the Temple manifested these differences. (Only those belonging to certain families, supposedly descended from Aaron, were eligible to be priests.) Those belonging to rich and distinguished Jewish families generally belonged to the sect or party of the *Sadducees*; they formed the dominant class and befriended the Romans, hoping to better their positions by so doing. Priests from more modest families, who faithfully carried out the priestly functions that were the source of their income, generally adhered to another sect, the *Pharisees*. Most of the Pharisees, however, were lay men, not priests.

The fundamental differences between the Sadducees and the Pharisees stemmed from the fact that the Sadducees accepted only the Law of Moses, the first five books of the Bible, as the religious

Zealots

Sadducees

norm. The Pharisees, however, also accepted the authority of the other books in what we call the Old Testament. The Pharisees also relied on an oral tradition for interpreting the sacred books.

The Sadducees denied the resurrection of the dead and the existence of angels, while the Pharisees affirmed these and other beliefs such as a universal judgment, heaven, and hell.

But the Pharisees had two main faults. First, through detailed rules they made the observance of the commandments more difficult, especially rest on the Sabbath day and ritual purification. Second, they prided themselves on their observance of the divine Law, and they tended to look down on others who did not observe it as they did. However, their observance was often merely external; the true spirit of the Law often escaped them. Most Jews did not respect the Sadducees because they were wealthier persons who worked closely with the Romans in order to maintain their comfortable place in society. Jesus tended to ignore the Sadducees and concentrated instead on reproving the Pharisees and warning the people against being taken in by the mere appearance of virtue.

The teachers of the Law and students of the sacred Scriptures, called *scribes*, also generally belonged to the Pharisaical party; these scribes

Essenes

were often called "rabbis," or teachers. Jesus, too, was often called rabbi.

The zealots made up another party or movement that existed among the Jews in the time of Jesus. They were zealous for the Jewish national religion and were prepared to defend it by force. While the Pharisees followed the path of compromise, waiting for better times, the zealots considered it absolutely intolerable that the People of God should be ruled by pagans. In the time of Jesus, the movement of the zealots was only at its very beginning; their activities would eventually culminate in the Jewish revolt of A.D. 66-70.

The *Essenes*, still another Jewish sect, had established a center in the desert near the Dead Sea. There they lived a strict community life of work and prayer. The Essenes did not go to the Temple; they did not recognize the authority of the priesthood that controlled Temple worship.

Pharisees

Priests

10 When Jesus started preaching,
John the Baptist
was calling people
to change their way of life
and be baptized.
Jesus came to be baptized.
This was a sign of his living
among sinful persons.
At Jesus' baptism,
God's Spirit showed
God's approval of Jesus.

In the fourteenth year of the reign of the emperor Tiberius, that is, around A.D. 27-28, John the Baptist (or John the Baptizer) appeared in the wilderness near Jericho. Up to that time the son of Zechariah had lived in a remote desert place and spent his time in prayer and fasting. His rough garment of camel's hair, similar to those of the ancient prophets, aroused the curiosity of the crowds. His message attracted even more attention: "Repent, for the kingdom of heaven is at hand" (Matthew 3:2).

People came from all over to hear John. He immersed them in the waters of the Jordan; those being baptized confessed their sins. This baptism was a symbol of an internal purification consisting of a profound change of heart, followed by a change in one's way of life in preparation for the coming of the Messiah.

John's message to the proud and self-satisfied was severe:

"You brood of vipers! Who warned you to flee from the wrath to come? Bear fruits that befit repentance, and do not begin to say to yourselves, 'We have Abraham as our father'; for I tell you, God is able from these stones to raise up children to Abraham. Even now the axe is

laid to the root of the trees; every tree therefore that does not bear good fruit is cut down and thrown into the fire." (Luke 3:7-9)

His counsel was less severe to simple people who came to ask what they should do; to them he replied with advice for helping the poor, "He who has two coats, let him share with him who has none; and he who has food, let him do likewise" (Luke 3:11).

The fame of this new prophet quickly spread throughout Judea and Galilee; he was venerated by the crowds. Many even asked whether John might not be the Messiah who was to come. In response, John repeated his own message and re-kindled expectations. He said, "I baptize you with water, but he who is mightier than I is coming, the thong of whose sandals I am not worthy to untie; he will baptize you with the Holy Spirit and with fire" (Luke 3:16).

The fame of John the Baptist was known as far away as Nazareth. Jesus knew that the time to begin his own mission was at hand. Saying good-bye to his mother (by then Joseph had been dead for some time), Jesus departed for the Jordan valley to be baptized by John the Baptist. When he arrived, a large number of people were awaiting their turn to be baptized. Jesus waited his turn along with the others—an innocent person among sinful persons in need of pardon.

When John saw Jesus, he was perplexed, "I need to be baptized by you, and do you come to me?" (Matthew 3:14). But Jesus insisted and John yielded. Jesus removed his garments and went down into the waters, and John baptized him; as Jesus bent over, John poured water on his head and shoulders. As Jesus emerged from the water, the heavens seemed to open above Jesus, and a white dove symbolizing the Holy Spirit descended upon his head. A mysterious voice from the heavens was heard to say: "This is my beloved Son, with whom I am well pleased" (Matthew 3:17).

Through this vision Jesus was encouraged for the new phase of his life, teaching people, before finally giving up his life to save humanity. Just as the dove in the story of Noah announced the appearance of a renewed world following the flood, the dove descending on Jesus at his baptism symbolized God's Spirit at work in Jesus. A new creation was to come into being through Jesus and in Jesus: the new People of God who were to be baptized in water and with the Holy Spirit.

11 After his baptism, Jesus
had a time of temptation.
In various ways Jesus
was tempted to use his life
for his own glory and pleasure,
rather than to obey God.

After his baptism by John, Jesus left and traveled towards the desert not far away. Only a few miles from the Jordan, beyond the oasis of Jericho, the Judean desert begins. It is a desert not of sand but of rocky hills. Jesus moved up among the rocks, going farther and farther away from other human beings to be alone with God and undisturbed in his prayers.

For forty days Jesus fasted and prayed. Moses had fasted and remained alone with God for forty days prior to receiving the tables of the Law through which he was to govern the People of God. Now Jesus knew the same experience of fasting and prayer prior to the beginning of his own ministry that would involve the creation of the new People of God.

However, after forty days he seemed just like another poor man suffering from hunger.

At this point a new personage little discussed in the Scriptures entered upon the scene: Satan, the Devil. "Satan" is the word in Hebrew for the one called "the Devil" in Greek. The word means "accuser," "defamer," or "slanderer." Satan is the spirit pictured as the source of evil and of the temptation to disobey God.

Then the Devil came to him and said, "If you are God's Son, order these stones to turn into bread."

But Jesus answered, "The scripture says, 'Man cannot live on bread alone, but needs every word that God speaks.'"

Then the Devil took Jesus to Jerusalem, the Holy City, set him on the highest point of the Temple, and said to him, "If you are God's Son, throw yourself down, for the scripture says,

'God will give orders to his
    angels about you;
they will hold you up with
    their hands,
so that not even your feet
    will be hurt on the
    stones.'"

Jesus answered, "But the scripture also says, 'Do not put the Lord your God to the test.'"

Then the Devil took Jesus to a very high mountain and showed him all the kingdoms of the world in all their greatness. "All this I will give you," the Devil said, "if you kneel down and worship me."

Then Jesus answered, "Go away, Satan! The scripture says, 'Worship the Lord your God and serve only him!'"

Then the Devil left Jesus; and angels came and helped him. (Matthew 4:3-11 TEV)

Andrew and John followed Jesus and asked him, "Rabbi . . . where are you staying?" (John 1:38). Jesus took them to the place where he was staying; they stayed with him that day, and he made a profound impression on them.

Later, Andrew brought his brother Simon to see Jesus. Jesus said to him, "Your name is Simon son of John, but you will be called Cephas." (This is the same as Peter and means "a rock.") (John 1:42 TEV) (The name Cephas is from the word for "rock" in Aramaic, the language Peter spoke. The name Peter is from the word for "rock" in Greek, the language the gospels were written in.)

Peter and Andrew came from Bethsaida, a fishing village on the shores of the Sea of Galilee. They had to leave the area where John was baptizing and return to Galilee, as did Jesus. There he met another fisherman of Bethsaida, Philip, who not only stayed with Jesus but wanted to introduce to Jesus his friend Nathanael, also called Bartholomew.

12 Jesus chose twelve men
to be his first disciples,
those closest to him.
These were to be
the leaders of the Church,
who were to share with others
the message of Jesus.

Upon his return from the desert, Jesus spent some time in the general area where John was baptizing. There he met for the first time some of those who would be among his first disciples. Two of them, Andrew and John, had followed John the Baptist. When John the Baptist saw Jesus again, he exclaimed, "Behold, the Lamb of God" (John 1:36). With this phrase he pointed to Jesus as the victim in a sacrifice—which Jesus would undergo on the cross.

another fisherman, Zebedee, mending nets in a boat with his two sons, James and John (this was the same John who had earlier met Jesus with Andrew). At the call of Jesus, James and John also left their nets and began to follow him.

Some time after that, in Capernaum, Jesus saw Levi, also called Matthew, who was a tax collector (or "publican"). Matthew was seated at the tax collector's stand. Jesus simply said, "Follow me" (Matthew 9:9), and Matthew got up and became one of his disciples.

Other disciples were attracted to Jesus and decided to follow him. Finally, after a night spent in prayer, Jesus selected twelve of these disciples to remain with him. They were Simon, called Peter; Andrew; James; John; Philip; Bartholomew; Thomas; Matthew; James, son of Alphaeus (or the Lesser); Thaddeus; Simon the Cananaean (or the Zealot); and Judas Iscariot, who would betray Jesus.

These twelve disciples were called "the Twelve" and, later, "the Apostles" or "those sent." This was because Jesus sent them out to announce the kingdom of God. In sending them out, he told them, "Take nothing with you for the trip: no walking stick, no beggar's bag, no food, no money, not even an extra shirt" (Luke 9:3 TEV). They were to depend solely upon God's care and upon the hospitality of good people.

Philip found Nathanael, and said to him, "We have found him of whom Moses in the law and also the prophets wrote, Jesus of Nazareth, the son of Joseph." Nathanael said to him, "Can anything good come out of Nazareth?" Philip said to him, "Come and see." Jesus saw Nathanael coming to him, and said of him, "Behold, an Israelite indeed, in whom is no guile!" Nathanael said to him, "How do you know me?" Jesus answered him, "Before Philip called you, when you were under the fig tree, I saw you." Nathanael answered him, "Rabbi, you are the Son of God! You are the King of Israel!"
(John 1:45-49)

These first contacts of Jesus with those who would be his closest disciples seem to have been irregular. Jesus was beginning to preach in Capernaum and in the other villages around the Sea of Galilee. They listened to him with admiration but then returned to their work.

One day, however, passing along the seashore, Jesus saw Simon (or Peter) fishing with his brother Andrew. Jesus said, "Come with me, and I will teach you to catch men" (Matthew 4:19 TEV). Peter and Andrew left their nets and decided to follow Jesus. Farther along the shore, Jesus saw

13 The first miracle of Jesus was changing water to wine at a wedding feast in Cana. Then, in the Temple he showed his authority by throwing out those changing money and selling animals for sacrifice.

Jesus had recently begun making the rounds of the towns and villages in Galilee, proclaiming his message: "The time is fulfilled, and the kingdom of God is at hand; repent, and believe in the gospel" (Mark 1:15).

Jesus announced good news: God truly loves humanity and the time has come when this love will be manifested in the Messiah.

In these early days of his mission Jesus and his disciples were invited to a wedding. This festive gathering of friends and relatives took place in Cana, a village not far from Nazareth. Mary, the mother of Jesus, was also invited. In the course of the banquet the wine ran out. Mary, who had been watching the serving, turned to Jesus and said, "They have no wine" (John 2:3).

And Jesus said to her, "O woman, what have you to do with me? My hour has not yet come." His mother said to the servants, "Do whatever he tells you." Now six stone jars were standing there, for the Jewish rites of purification, each holding twenty or thirty gallons. Jesus said to them, "Fill the jars with water." And they filled them up to the brim. He said to them, "Now draw some out, and take it to the steward of the feast." So they took it. When the steward of the feast tasted the water now become wine, and did not know where it came from (though the servants who had drawn the water knew),

the steward of the feast called the bridegroom and said to him, "Every man serves the good wine first; and when men have drunk freely, then the poor wine; but you have kept the good wine until now." (John 2:4-10)

This first miracle performed by Jesus was an act of goodness towards the new married couple to avoid spoiling the joy of the occasion. At the same time, it was a symbolic gesture. The new wine, from water used for Jewish rites of purification, was the symbol of the divine love and forgiveness that would be fully manifested in the "hour" that Jesus indicated: the hour of his death on the cross and his subsequent glorification. Jesus' preaching and miracles already point to these saving acts.

Not long after that came the time of the Jewish Passover. Jesus, as was his custom, went down to Jerusalem with the usual large number of pil-

grims. In the porticoes of the Temple, Jesus found merchants selling oxen, sheep, and doves for the sacrifices and also money changers who exchanged foreign money for the Temple offerings. Jesus had seen such disgraceful commercialism many times in the Temple; but this time he decided to act with the authority of a Messiah. He fashioned himself a whip out of cords and began to chase the merchants out of the Temple along with their sheep and oxen. He overturned the tables of the money changers. To those who sold doves or pigeons (sacrifices made by the poorest people), he said, "Take them out of here! Stop making my Father's house a marketplace!" (John 2:16 TEV).

Then Jesus spoke mysteriously about his future resurrection: "Destroy this Temple, and in three days I will raise it up" (John 2:19). The evangelist John adds, "He spoke of the temple of his body" (John 2:21). At the time no one understood.

14

A Pharisee named Nicodemus
came to Jesus secretly.
Jesus told him about the need
for a new kind of life,
for being born again.
A Samaritan woman met Jesus
at a well. He told her
he could satisfy
her deepest thirst.

During a week that Jesus spent in Jerusalem celebrating the Passover, a prominent Pharisee named Nicodemus, a teacher of the Law, was very impressed by the authority with which Jesus taught and by the miracles he performed. To avoid possible criticism from his fellow Pharisees, Nicodemus came to see Jesus at night, so no one knew of his visit.

Nicodemus believed Jesus was an authentic teacher sent by God, but he wished to know more about Jesus' teaching. Jesus was willing to explain everything to Nicodemus, but first he wanted to shake the Pharisee's confidence in his own learning.

Jesus answered him, "Truly, truly, I say to you, unless one is born anew, he cannot see the kingdom of God." Nicodemus said to him, "How can a man be born when he is old? Can he enter a second time into his mother's womb and be born?" (John 3:3-4)

Jesus replied that the rebirth was spiritual through "water and the Spirit" (John 3:5), that is to say, through baptism. This rebirth would be into a new kind of life, "eternal life," given by the Holy Spirit. All this was to be the result of the love of God:

For God so loved the world that he gave his only Son, that whoever believes in him should not perish but have eternal life. (John 3:16)

Nicodemus was not able to understand all this, but he continued to be attracted by Jesus; later he would defend Jesus before the Sanhedrin and assist Joseph of Arimathea in arranging for the burial of Jesus after his crucifixion.

Jesus then left Jerusalem and Judea and started back toward Galilee. He had to go through Samaria. Near a city called Sychar he stopped to rest by a well since he was tired from the journey. The disciples had gone away into the city to buy food. A Samaritan woman carrying a jar came to the well to draw water. Jesus asked her for a drink of water.

The Samaritan woman was amazed at this request. The Jews considered the Samaritans impure, like Gentiles; for this reason, anything offered by a Samaritan, such as water, would have been considered impure. The woman asked, "How is it that you, a Jew, ask a drink of me, a woman of Samaria?" (John 4:9).

At this time it was unheard of for a rabbi to speak to a woman in public—especially to a Samaritan woman. However, throughout all of his public ministry Jesus showed an enlightened attitude toward women. The woman was willing to talk to Jesus, and after this encounter she became a witness to her people that Jesus was "the Savior of the world."

Jesus said to her that if she had known whom she was talking to she would have asked him for "living water" that would satisfy the thirst for eternal life. However, the woman did not understand and continued to speak of ordinary water to satisfy ordinary thirst—the water that could be drawn from the well. Jesus had to explain again, and then the woman asked for that living water.

Instead, Jesus told the woman to go bring her husband there. She replied, "I have no husband" (John 4:17). At this point Jesus unveiled the woman's own life to her, "You are right in saying 'I have no husband'; for you have had five husbands, and he whom you have now is not your husband" (John 4:17-18).

The woman then understood that Jesus was a prophet. She then asked him a religious question:

"Our fathers worshiped on this mountain; and you say that in Jerusalem is the place where men ought to worship." Jesus said to her, "Woman, believe me, the hour is coming when neither on this mountain nor in Jerusalem will you worship the Father. You worship what you do not know; we worship what we know, for salvation is from the Jews. But the hour is coming, and now is, when the true worshipers will worship the Father in spirit and truth, for such the Father seeks to worship him. God is spirit, and those who worship him must worship in spirit and truth." The woman said to him, "I know that Messiah is coming (he who is called Christ); when he comes, he will show us all things." Jesus said to her, "I who speak to you am he." (John 4:20-26)

The Samaritan woman believed. She left her water jar and ran back into the city to tell all the people to come to see "the Savior of the world" (John 4:42).

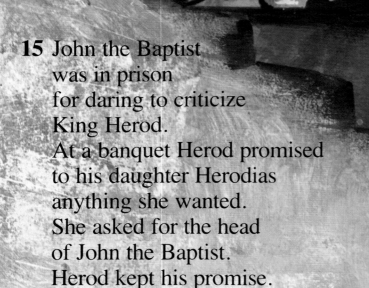

15 John the Baptist
was in prison
for daring to criticize
King Herod.
At a banquet Herod promised
to his daughter Herodias
anything she wanted.
She asked for the head
of John the Baptist.
Herod kept his promise.

Jesus and his disciples were now journeying throughout Galilee and Judea, preaching and healing. People were flocking to Jesus from everywhere. The disciples of John the Baptist began to be concerned, as if Jesus were in competition with John. So they complained to John. These complaints gave rise to the selfless witness of John the Baptist:

> "You yourselves bear me witness, that I said, I am not the Christ, but I have been sent before him. He who has the bride is the bridegroom; the friend of the bridegroom, who stands and hears him, rejoices greatly at the bridegroom's voice; therefore this joy of mine is now full. He must increase, but I must decrease."
>
> (John 3:28-30)

The coming of the Messiah was thus compared to a wedding feast: Jesus was the bridegroom and John merely the best man, who had helped to prepare the feast but whose role was now to draw back.

Shortly afterwards, John was arrested by Herod Antipas, the tetrarch of Galilee, and confined in a fortress east of the Dead Sea. John had had the courage to confront Herod and rebuke him for the scandal of having married the wife of his brother Philip, who was living in Rome. Her name was Herodias. She hated John bitterly and wanted Herod to have him executed, but the tetrarch hesitated. Even while he was in prison, John was able to receive his disciples there.

Aware that his days were numbered, though, John one day sent some of his disciples to Jesus to ask, perhaps for their reassurance,

"Are you he who is to come, or shall we look for another?" And Jesus answered them, "Go and tell John what you hear and see: the blind receive their sight and the lame walk, lepers are cleansed and the deaf hear, and the dead are raised up, and the poor have good news preached to them. And blessed is he who takes no offense at me." (Matthew 11:3-6)

Herodias continued to wait for the right moment when she could bring about the execution of John. The occasion came at a birthday banquet for Herod Antipas that was held at the summer residence of the tetrarch near where John lay in prison. Herod, along with many officials, dined in a separate hall from the women, in accordance with the custom of the time. The wine was beginning to have its effect. Herodias had her beautiful young daughter from her first marriage, Salome, sent in to dance for the company. Salome was an accomplished dancer and won the admiration of Herod with her performance:

> For when Herodias' daughter came in and danced, she pleased Herod and his guests; and the king said to the girl, "Ask me for whatever you wish, and I will grant it." And he vowed to her, "Whatever you ask me, I will give you, even half of my kingdom." And she went out, and said to her mother, "What shall I ask?" And she said, "The head of John the baptizer."
>
> (Mark 6:22-25)

Herod was very sorry about his promise, but he feared the criticism of his guests if he would break his promise. So he sent a guard to the prison with orders to cut off John's head and to bring it back on a platter. Shortly after, the bloody head of the prophet was carried into the dining hall. The guard gave it to Salome, who took it to Herodias. Herodias succeeded in getting her way.

The disciples of John the Baptist recovered his body and buried it with honor. Thus John ended his prophetic career as a martyr.

16 The miracles of Jesus—
curing the sick and
freeing people from demons—
were signs of the power of God
now working in the world.

With its farms and towns and its fishing villages around the Sea of Galilee, Galilee was for about a year Jesus' main field of activity. He both taught and performed miracles. People brought him the sick on stretchers. The deaf, the blind, epileptics, and those possessed by demons all came; the latter acted very strangely, moved from within by spirits. In ancient times people thought sickness was caused by evil spirits. Jesus cured the sick and cured those who were thus possessed. In doing this, he not only showed his goodness and compassion; he also proclaimed by these actions that he was fighting against Satan. Rather, the rule of God had begun in Jesus himself.

The first chapters of the Gospel of Mark present typical activity for Jesus. Jesus was in Capernaum on the Sabbath day. The Jews met in the synagogue to pray and to hear the reading of Scripture. Jesus and his disciples also entered the synagogue, and Jesus taught those gathered there. Suddenly there was a hoarse cry: "What have you to do with us, Jesus of Nazareth? Have you come to destroy us? I know who you are, the Holy One of God" (Mark 1:24).

The gospels say that it was an "unclean spirit," who spoke through the mouth of an unfortunate person who was possessed.

Jesus rebuked the evil spirit: "Be silent, and come out of him!" (Mark 1:25).

There was a howl of pain. The man's body became contorted. Then, suddenly, he was free and restored to a normal state, amid the fear and amazement of those around him.

Jesus went out of the synagogue and entered the house of the brothers Simon and Andrew. They were natives of Bethsaida, but had moved to Capernaum, about three miles away. Inside the house the mother-in-law of Simon was ill with a fever. Jesus took her by the hand and raised her up. She felt completely cured and began to prepare a meal for Jesus and his disciples.

When evening fell and the Sabbath was over, a crowd gathered at the door. Jesus cured the sick and freed the possessed among them until it was late. After a brief night's rest, Jesus arose while it was still dark and went away to a deserted spot to pray. When they realized that he was no longer in the house, Peter and the other disciples came to look for him. They said to him, "Every one is searching for you" (Mark 1:37).

However, Jesus wished to visit other villages to preach there. During his journey he met a leper along the road, who recognized him and threw himself down on his knees before him, crying out, "If you will, you can make me clean" (Mark 1:40). According to Jewish custom, persons suffering from the illness of leprosy were considered unclean, and other Jews were supposed to avoid them. But Jesus, moved by the man's plight, reached out and touched the man and said, "I will; be clean" (Mark 1:41). The man's leprosy immediately disappeared.

Jesus returned to Capernaum after a few days. Once again the crowds flocked around his door. Jesus preached to them. Four men arrived carrying a paralyzed man on a stretcher, but they were not able to get close to Jesus because of the crowd. So they went up on the roof, removed the portion of the roof above Jesus, and lowered the man down in front of him. Seeing their faith, Jesus said to the paralyzed man, "My son, your sins are forgiven" (Mark 2:5).

Some of the teachers of the Law, shocked at this, asked, "Who can forgive sins but God alone?" (Mark 2:7).

Jesus answered, "I will prove to you, then, that the Son of Man has authority on earth to forgive sins. . . . I tell you, get up, pick up your mat, and go home!" (Mark 2:10 TEV).

The man rose, took up his mat, and left—to the amazement of all. "We never saw anything like this," they said (Mark 2:12).

17 In the Sermon on the Mount
Jesus described
life among persons
whose lives are ruled by God.

One day Jesus was followed by a crowd, many of whom had come from far away to hear him. He went up on a hill overlooking the Sea of Galilee, and sat down with his own disciples and the crowd. He began to teach them about the kind of life his followers should lead and how they should face the difficult situations in their lives.

This collection of teachings commonly is called the Sermon on the Mount. Here are some examples of the teachings of Jesus as given in this famous sermon.

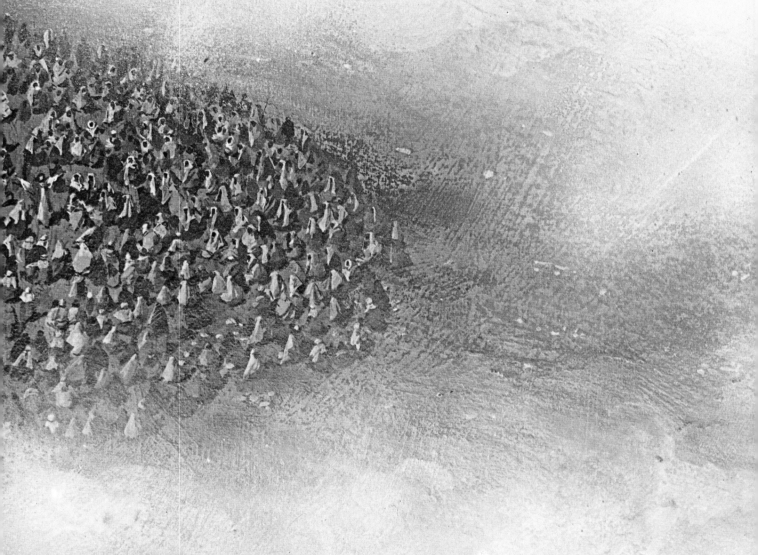

The Golden Rule

"Do for others what you want them to do for you: this is the meaning of the Law of Moses and of the teachings of the prophets."

(Matthew 7:12 TEV)

Right Conduct, Not Just Appearance

"Beware of practicing your piety before men in order to be seen by them; for then you will have no reward from your Father who is in heaven." (Matthew 6:1)

Love of Enemies

"You have heard that it was said, 'You shall love your neighbor and hate your enemy.' But I say to you, Love your enemies and pray for those who persecute you, so that you may be sons of your Father who is in heaven; for he makes his sun rise on the evil and on the good, and sends rain on the just and on the unjust. For if you love those who love you, what reward have you? Do not even the tax collectors do the same? And if you salute only your brethren, what more are you doing than others? Do not even the Gentiles do the same? You, therefore, must be perfect, as your heavenly Father is perfect." (Matthew 5:43-48)

The Beatitudes

"Blessed are the poor in spirit, for theirs is the kingdom of heaven.

"Blessed are those who mourn, for they shall be comforted.

"Blessed are the meek, for they shall inherit the earth.

"Blessed are those who hunger and thirst for righteousness, for they shall be satisfied.

"Blessed are the merciful, for they shall obtain mercy.

"Blessed are the pure in heart, for they shall be called sons of God.

"Blessed are those who are persecuted for righteousness' sake, for theirs is the kingdom of heaven.

"Blessed are you when men revile you and persecute you and utter all kinds of evil against you falsely on my account. Rejoice and be glad, for your reward is great in heaven, for so men persecuted the prophets who were before you." (Matthew 5:3-12)

Non-violence

"You have heard that it was said, 'An eye for an eye and a tooth for a tooth.' But I say to you, Do not resist one who is evil. But if any one strikes you on the right cheek, turn to him the other also; and if any one would sue you and take your coat, let him have your cloak as well; and if any one forces you to go one mile, go with him two miles. Give to him who begs from you, and do not refuse him who would borrow from you." (Matthew 5:38-42)

True Riches

"Do not lay up for yourselves treasures on earth, where moth and rust consume and where thieves break in and steal, but lay up for yourselves treasures in heaven, where neither moth nor rust consumes and where thieves do not break in and steal. For where your treasure is, there will your heart be also. . . .

"No one can serve two masters; for either he will hate the one and love the other, or he will be devoted to the one and despise the other. You cannot serve God and mammon."

(Matthew 6:19-21,24)

18 The activity of Jesus shows the importance of trusting God, the compassion of Jesus, and his authority to forgive sins.

Galilee, the northern part of Palestine, was Jesus' home. There he grew up; there he began his preaching; there he performed his first miracles. Here are three of these miracles as recorded by Luke.

Capernaum was a city on the northwestern shore of the Sea of Galilee where Jesus established himself at the beginning of his public mission. There lived in the city, in addition to Jews, a number of foreigners, including a detachment of Roman soldiers. One Roman officer, a centurion, prompted Jesus to perform an important miracle. This centurion was an admirer of the Jewish religion; he helped support the synagogue at Capernaum, and, no doubt, he had heard about Jesus. When one of his servants became gravely ill, he sent the elders of the Jews to ask Jesus to intervene.

Several friends brought a message from the centurion to Jesus: "Lord, do not trouble yourself, for I am not worthy to have you come under my roof; therefore I did not presume to come to you. But say the word, and let my servant be healed" (Luke 7:6-7). This Roman officer had understood the central importance of *faith* and trust in God. Jesus praised the faith of the centurion and healed his servant.

Also in Galilee, near Nazareth, there was a town called Nain. Jesus, accompanied by his disciples, was going there to preach when they met a crowd coming out of the town. It was a funeral procession for a widow's only son, who had died at a very young age. When Jesus saw the widow, he was moved with pity. He said to her, "Do not weep," and then he touched the coffin with his hand and said, "Young man, I say to you, arise" (Luke 7:13-14). And the young man arose. This miracle was performed as a result of the mercy and compassion of Jesus.

Jesus was becoming well known because of these things. On another occasion a Pharisee named Simon invited Jesus to dinner. Jesus was comfortably seated at the low semi-circular table on which people ate in those times when a woman ap-

proached him. We know very little about this un-named woman. Luke's version of the story pic-tures her as a sinner, but other versions in Mark and Matthew do not. She began to wash his feet with her tears, dry them with her hair, and anoint them with the ointment she had brought.

She was humiliating herself and repenting for her sin. However, the host, a proud and skeptical man, thought to himself, "If this man were truly a prophet he would know what sort of woman was wiping his feet with her hair." Jesus called him over and said, "Simon, I have something to say to you." The Pharisee replied, "What is it, Teacher?" (Luke 7:40).

"A certain creditor had two debtors; one owed five hundred denarii, and the other fifty. When they could not pay, he forgave them both. Now which of them will love him more?" Simon answered, "The one, I suppose, to whom he forgave more." And he said to him, "You have judged rightly." Then turning toward the woman he said to Simon, "Do you see this woman? I entered your house, you gave me no water for my feet, but she has wet my feet with her tears and wiped them with her hair. . . . Therefore I tell you, her sins, which are many, are for-given, for she loved much; but he who is for-given little, loves little." And he said to her, "Your sins are forgiven."

(Luke 7:41-44, 47-48)

This was a very serious statement by Jesus. Only God could forgive sins. Jesus was then and there indirectly claiming to be God, to the amaze-ment and even scandal of the other guests; but this did not bother Jesus. Turning to the woman, he said, "Your faith has saved you; go in peace" (Luke 7:50).

In Mark's version of the story Jesus praised the woman and said of this anointing, "And truly I say to you, wherever the gospel is preached in the whole world, what she has done will be told in memory of her" (Mark 14:9).

Jesus was not a trickster or a magician. The miracles he performed were signs of the salvation that he came into the world to bring. So before a miracle Jesus usually demanded a profession of faith, to show that the external miracle was only the confirmation of the even greater miracle of faith that had occurred inside the person. Faith is the indispensable starting point for anyone wish-ing to become one of his followers.

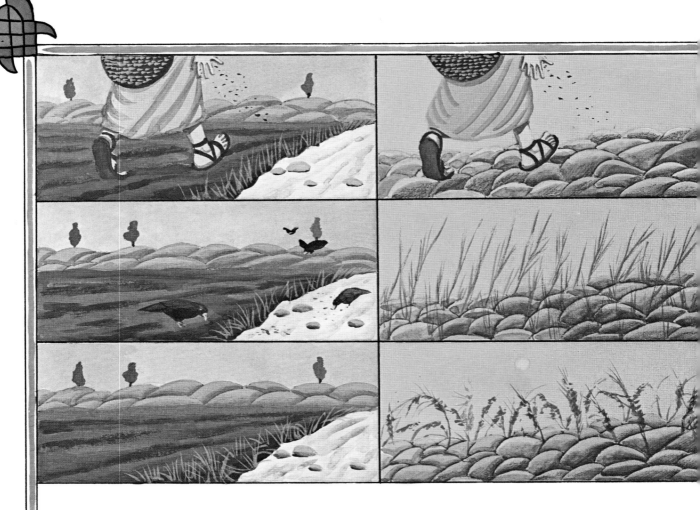

19
The parable of the sower
describes the response
of different persons
to Jesus' message about God.
It tells about some seeds
that produce fruit
and others that don't.

Jesus spoke the language and shared the culture of that time and of that country. So, like the Jewish rabbis of his time, he taught by using parables.

Parables were stories that used the details of daily life to teach religious truths. One of the purposes of these parables was to make the teaching more lively and direct. Often parables have a surprise ending. Jesus frequently made use of parables. His parables show that he was a remarkable observer both of the details of daily life and of the human heart.

Among the many parables of Jesus recorded in the gospels, one of the best known and most beautiful is the parable of the sower. According to the evangelist Mark, Jesus was seated in a boat when he told this parable; a crowd stood on the shore listening to him. Here is the parable:

"Listen! Once there was a man who went out to sow grain. As he scattered the seed in the field, some of it fell along the path, and the birds came and ate it up. Some of it fell on rocky ground, where there was little soil. The seeds soon sprouted, because the soil wasn't deep. Then, when the sun came up, it burned the young plants; and because the roots had

not grown deep enough, the plants soon dried up. Some of the seed fell among thorn bushes, which grew up and choked the plants, and they didn't bear grain. But some seeds fell in good soil, and the plants sprouted, grew, and bore grain: some had thirty grains, others sixty, and others one hundred.'' (Mark 4:3-8 TEV)

This, then, is the parable. Jesus concluded it with the words, "Listen, then, if you have ears" (Mark 4:9 TEV). Jesus was calling persons to listen to the parable, to accept it, and to put it into practice.

In the gospel account, Mark puts the words of explanation of the parable in the mouth of Jesus. However, the interpretation is very likely a later reflection on the parable by the early Christians. The seeds sown on the path are those who hear God's message without understanding; Satan comes immediately and takes the Word away from them. The seeds sown on rocky ground are those who are not dependable; they hear the message with joy, but when difficulties or persecutions come, they abandon it because it has not taken deep root in them. The seeds sown among thorns are those who hear the message but then become busy with the cares of the world; they would like to follow the message but their desire to do so is choked out by other desires for power or riches. Finally, the seeds planted in good soil are those who hear the message, understand it, and put it into practice. These last "bear fruit, thirtyfold and sixtyfold and a hundredfold" (Mark 4:20).

The parable of the sower is a powerful call to hear and put into practice the message of Jesus. It is not enough merely to hear it absentmindedly; it is necessary to meditate upon it and allow it to grow deep roots in one's heart. If that happens, it will bear abundant fruit.

This parable illustrates the confidence Jesus had in his own preaching. At the same time, his mention of infertile ground encouraged the first disciples and the first missionaries. They needed to understand that not everyone who heard them would be converted. They had to continue to proclaim the teaching of the Master in the conviction that whoever heard it with an open heart would accept it, put it into practice, and bear much fruit.

20 Jesus stilled a stormy sea
when he and his disciples
were in a boat.
He freed a man
from many evil spirits.

Peter no longer had time to practice his trade as a fisherman. Because he was able to use Peter's boat, Jesus could visit the towns and villages around the Sea of Galilee more easily. (The Sea of Galilee is about seven miles across and thirteen miles long.) One day, after he had preached from the boat to the people on the shore, Jesus asked Peter to cross to the other side of the lake. The disciples were with him in the boat.

While they were out on the open sea, a great storm arose. With the sails lowered, the boat was at the mercy of the waves; stirred up by the high winds, the waves came crashing over the sides of the fragile craft. Jesus was sleeping in the back of the boat. Terrified, the disciples awoke him. "Teacher, don't you care that we are about to die?" they asked him (Mark 4:38 TEV).

Jesus stood up and commanded the wind, "Be quiet!" and he said to the waves, "Be still!" The wind died down, and there was a great calm. Then Jesus said to his disciples, "Why are you frightened? Do you still have no faith?"

But they were terribly afraid and began to say to one another, "Who is this man? Even the wind and the waves obey him!"

(Mark 4:39-41 TEV)

When they had arrived on the other shore, they got out of the boat and started up the slopes of the territory belonging to the Gerasenes. Gerasa was one of the cities of the Decapolis; the majority of people there were Gentiles, not Jews.

Suddenly they were confronted by a crazed man, almost naked, who charged about beating his chest with stones. He was a demoniac, or possessed man, whom no one had ever succeeded in taming or controlling. Even when bound with chains, he always succeeded in breaking them and returning to live wildly in the caves on the shore. The man cried out to Jesus, "Jesus, Son of the Most High God! What do you want with me? For God's sake, I beg you, don't punish me!"

So Jesus asked him, "What is your name?"

The man answered, "My name is 'Mob'—there are so many of us!" (Mark 5:7,9 TEV).

There was a herd of pigs grazing there on the hillside. Jesus commanded the unclean spirits to leave the man; but they begged Jesus to be allowed to remain in that country. "Send us to the pigs, let us go into them," they said to Jesus (Mark 5:12 TEV).

Jesus agreed, but when the unclean spirits entered into the pigs, the animals rushed down the steep ravine and drowned themselves in the sea. There were around two thousand of them. Terrified, the men who cared for the pigs went into the city to tell the inhabitants what had happened. People came and found the man who formerly had been possessed both sane and calm, but they wished to have nothing to do with Jesus and begged him to leave.

Peter

James

21

Jesus sent out apostles to tell about God's rule. Jesus warned them to expect persecution.

Bartholomew

Jesus moved through towns and villages, preaching in the synagogues, in public squares, and in remote open fields—wherever he could gather a crowd to listen. He healed the sick who were brought to him. The most profound miseries that he witnessed, however, were those of the poor people, who groaned under the yoke of oppression. The Pharisees and the teachers of the Law looked down on the poor because their hard life did not permit them either to know or to practice the fine points taught as an integral part of the Law of Moses. Once Jesus was talking about the teachers of the Law: "They tie onto people's backs loads that are heavy and hard to carry, yet they aren't willing even to lift a finger to help them carry those loads. . . . How terrible for you, teachers of the Law and Pharisees! You hypocrites! You lock the door to the Kingdom of heaven in people's faces. . . ." (Matthew 23:4,13 TEV).

Because the people lacked real leadership from their official leaders, Jesus "had compassion for them, because they were harassed and helpless, like sheep without a

Simon
the Zealot

James son of Alphaeus

Andrew

John

Matthew

shepherd'' (Matthew 9:36). Jesus told his disciples, ''The harvest is plentiful, but the laborers are few; pray therefore the Lord of the harvest to send out laborers into his harvest'' (Matthew 9:37).

Jesus had chosen twelve apostles who were with him continually. The time had now come for them to help in making known the good news. Jesus gave the apostles power to heal every sort of illness and to cast out demons; then he sent them out in pairs to towns and villages to preach.

This mission was to prepare the apostles for the time after his resurrection when they would be sent to preach not only to their fellow Jews, but also to the rest of the world. (The word *apostle* means ''sent.'') Jesus gave them instructions that would apply to their mission later, when they would be faced with actual persecution:

> ''Behold, I send you out as sheep in the midst of wolves; so be wise as serpents and innocent as doves. Beware of men; for they will deliver you up to councils, and flog you in their synagogues, and you will be dragged before governors and kings for my sake, to bear testimony before them and the Gentiles. When they deliver you up, do not be anxious how you are to speak or what you are to say; for what you are to say will be given to you in that hour; for it is not you who speak, but the Spirit of your Father speaking through you.''
>
> (Matthew 10:16-20)

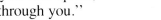

Philip

Thomas

Thaddeus

Judas

The word "Messiah" occurs many times in this book and in the Bible as a whole. If we want to understand Jesus, we need to understand what we mean by Messiah. The disciples of Jesus and the evangelists tried to understand and express who Jesus was. The best way they found was to say that he was the Messiah, the expected Savior-King of Israel.

Against the background of the Old Testament, Jesus acted as a new Elijah, a new Moses, the shepherd who would gather and feed his flock, the Messiah who would save his people.

Once again we find ourselves along the shores of the Sea of Galilee. The disciples had just returned from their missionary journey. Another huge crowd had gathered. Yet the disciples were tired. Sensitive to their condition, Jesus said, "Come away by yourselves to a lonely place, and rest a while" (Mark 6:31).

22 Jesus multiplied loaves
and fishes to feed a crowd
of five thousand people.
The crowd represented
the new People of God,
led by Jesus,
as the old People of God
was led by Moses.

They got into a boat, but the crowd noticed them doing it, guessed where they were going, and beat them there on land; the numbers of the crowd had increased, with people coming from all the neighboring towns. When Jesus and the disciples landed, there was a great throng standing before them. Seeing all the people, Jesus was moved with compassion for them. He began to teach them.

He spoke for a long time; his words were so fascinating that nobody noticed the passage of time. The disciples were the first to notice; they came to Jesus and said,

"This is a lonely place, and the hour is now late; send them away, to go into the country and villages round about and buy themselves something to eat." But he answered them, "You give them something to eat." And they said to him, "Shall we go and buy two hundred denarii worth of bread, and give it to them to eat?" And he said to them, "How many loaves have you? Go and see." And when they had found out, they said, "Five, and two fish." Then he commanded them all to sit down by companies upon the green grass. So they sat down in groups, by hundreds and by fifties. (Mark 6:35-40)

Five loaves and two fish were, of course, a ridiculously small amount of food for this huge throng. But the new People of God was gathered. Jesus, aided by the disciples, was about to feed them in green fields, just as Moses had fed their ancestors in the desert. Jesus raised his eyes to heaven and spoke the blessing on the loaves and fishes. He broke the bread and gave it to his disciples, and they in turn distributed it to the people.

The food which Jesus provided was so abundant that there was a great deal left over. "And they took up twelve baskets full of broken pieces, and of the fish. And those who ate the loaves were five thousand men" (Mark 6:43-44).

23 Jesus said,
"I am the bread of life."
He came to give real life,
fellowship with God.
The Eucharist, or Communion,
is one opportunity
for this.

On one occasion, after the miraculous multiplying of the loaves and fishes, Jesus found himself again surrounded by a crowd. They had eaten the bread that had been miraculously produced, but they did not understand that it was really a sign: It was God's seal of approval upon his Son, to show that Jesus' mission was authentic. People seeing such a sign should have believed in Jesus. However, many still did not have faith in him.

Some people—whom John the evangelist called "the Jews"—came to Jesus and told him that to believe in him they needed to see an overwhelming sign, a sign such as their ancestors had seen when Moses fed them manna in the desert. "What sign do you do, that we may see, and believe you?" the Jews asked Jesus. "What work do you perform? Our fathers ate the manna in the wilderness; as it is written, 'He gave them bread from heaven to eat'" (John 6:30-31).

This question gave Jesus the opportunity to teach his questioners. He declared that he himself was the Bread of Life come down from heaven to give "eternal life" to human beings. By "eternal life," Jesus meant true communion with God, a communion that could not be interrupted even by death. Jesus explained that the Eucharist or Holy Communion would be an opportunity for persons to enjoy union with him and with God the Father. Here are the most important parts of his talk at Capernaum:

"I am the bread of life," Jesus told them. "He who comes to me will never be hungry; he who believes in me will never be thirsty. Now, I told you that you have seen me but will not believe. Everyone whom my Father gives me will come to me. I will never turn away anyone who comes to me, . . . For what my Father wants is that all who see the Son and believe in him should have eternal life. And I will raise them to life on the last day. . . . Stop grumbling among yourselves. No one can come to me unless the Father who sent me draws him to me; . . . I am the living bread that came down from heaven. If anyone eats this bread, he will live forever. The bread that I will give him is my flesh, which I give so that the world may live."

This started an angry argument among them. "How can this man give us his flesh to eat?" they asked.

Jesus said to them, "I am telling you the truth: if you do not eat the flesh of the Son of Man and drink his blood, you will not have life in yourselves. Whoever eats my flesh and drinks my blood has eternal life, and I will raise him to life on the last day. For my flesh is the real food; my blood is the real drink. Whoever eats my flesh and drinks my blood lives in me, and I live in him. The living Father sent me, and because of him I live also. In the same way whoever eats me will live because of me. This, then, is the bread that came down from heaven; it is not like the bread that your ancestors ate, but then later died. The one who eats this bread will live forever."

(John 6:35-37,40,43-44,51-58 TEV)

Many of the followers of Jesus who had more worldly or nationalistic views about the Messiah became disillusioned with Jesus. They considered this teaching of Jesus a "hard saying" to believe.

Jesus said to the twelve, "Do you also wish to go away?" Simon Peter answered him, "Lord, to whom shall we go? You have the words of eternal life; and we have believed and have come to know, that you are the Holy One of God."

(John 6:67-69)

24 At Caesarea Philippi
Peter became the first disciple
to say clearly to Jesus,
"You are the Messiah,
the Son of the living God."

Jesus came into this world to speak to the heart of every person—and to save everyone. He knew, however, that words alone would never be enough; only the testimony of his whole life would be convincing. His plan was to commit his teachings, the example of his life, and, most of all, his love to certain chosen followers, his disciples. They would form the community of his followers, who would proclaim the living message of Jesus in the years and the centuries to come. So Jesus dedicated a large part of his public life to the training of the men and women whom he had chosen as his friends.

Jesus was passing near Caesarea Philippi with his disciples. Not long before, Philip, a grandson of Herod the Great, had enlarged and beautified the city and dedicated it to Caesar Augustus. Suddenly Jesus asked his disciples directly, "Who do people say the Son of Man is?" (Matthew 16:13 TEV). The disciples were embarrassed by the question. There were so many opinions about Jesus.

Jesus spoke with the authority of the prophets. Like the prophets, he performed marvelous works. People compared him with other heroes in the history of Israel. Some thought Elijah had come back to life in Jesus; others thought of Jeremiah, or even of John the Baptist, whom King Herod had so recently beheaded.

Jesus listened to the various uncertain replies that his disciples gave to his question. Then he asked them, "But who do *you* say that I am?" (Matthew 16:15).

They were silent. It was one thing to repeat the gossip of others about Jesus. It was something else to express their own convictions.

But then Simon Peter exclaimed to Jesus, "You are the Messiah, the Son of the living God" (Matthew 16:16 TEV).

And Jesus answered him, "Blessed are you, Simon Bar-Jona! For flesh and blood has not revealed this to you, but my Father who is in heaven. And I tell you, you are Peter, and on this rock I will build my church, and the powers of death shall not prevail against it."
(Matthew 16:17-18)

What is clear in this passage is that Peter was the rock on which the Church was to be built; but how he would be the foundation is not clear. Roman Catholic Christians believe Jesus was choosing Peter, who would later become the bishop of Rome, and his successors as bishops there, to head the Church. Most Protestant Christians believe that Jesus' response to Peter's profession meant that the Church would be built on the faith that Jesus is the Messiah, the Son of the living God. Peter was the first to confess so clearly who Jesus is.

25 Jesus warned his disciples
that he would suffer,
be put to death,
and be raised from the dead.
On Mount Tabor those closest
to Jesus saw him
wonderfully changed
and talking with Moses
and Elijah.
This was a kind of preview
of his resurrection.

After Peter's profession of faith, Jesus grew closer to his disciples; he began to explain to them even more difficult aspects of his teaching.

People of those days who were expecting the Messiah—the Savior—hoped for a powerful worldly kingdom. The Messiah was to rule over this kingdom, surrounded with power and glory.

Jesus, however, intended to save persons by working from within. That is why he became human, sharing everything with us except sin, sharing especially in our sufferings.

Jesus had to begin to explain to his chosen followers that he would have to suffer. All the disciples, even Peter, rejected what Jesus was saying. They could not accept that such a wise and powerful Master as Jesus should suffer and die like a common criminal. Jesus also spoke mysteriously of a resurrection to come after his death. But the meaning of this was not clear, and it did not make up for the disgrace toward which Jesus said he was headed.

Jesus wanted to encourage the faith of those nearest and dearest to him. So one day he took Peter, James, and John and went off to climb Mount Tabor, a beautiful mountain in southern Galilee. When they had reached the summit, Jesus began to pray. As he prayed, he was transfigured, or changed, before the three apostles. His face shone like the sun, and his garments became as white as pure light.

Then two important figures of the Old Testament appeared beside him and began to talk with him. The two figures were Moses, who had liberated his people from slavery in Egypt, and Elijah, the fiery prophet from the days of the kings of Israel.

Moses and Elijah talked with Jesus and spoke of his death and resurrection. Peter, James, and John had fallen down on the ground and believed they were dreaming. Peter, hardly realizing himself what he was saying, spoke up:

And Peter said to Jesus, "Lord, it is well that we are here; if you wish, I will make three booths here, one for you and one for Moses and one for Elijah." He was still speaking, when lo, a bright cloud overshadowed them, and a voice from the cloud said, "This is my beloved Son, with whom I am well pleased; listen to him."
(Matthew 17:4-5)

At this the disciples were filled with awe. When they came to themselves, Jesus alone was still in front of them, and his appearance had returned to normal. As they went down the mountain, Jesus told them not to reveal what they had seen until he had risen from the dead.

In the later memory of the three apostles, the transfiguration of Jesus came to have great significance. By coming into this world, Jesus gave to everyone and everything a new significance. With the resurrection of Jesus, the glory of God would truly manifest itself on earth. Through the Church of Christ the world itself would slowly become transformed.

26 When Jesus taught, he talked about everyday events and common objects. Jesus welcomed children and even used them as examples for adults.

Jesus took advantage of everything that happened, large or small, to help his disciples look at themselves, at others, and at life in the new way. He paid particular attention to children. He was not only concerned about how children were to be treated; he also wanted to show how adults could learn from them.

On one occasion when children were brought to Jesus, the disciples were annoyed. Like so many adults, they were often brusque and impatient with children. They thought Jesus had more important things to do than to spend time with children. Jesus rebuked them for this attitude: "Let the children come to me, do not hinder them; for to such belongs the kingdom of God. Truly, I say to you, whoever does not receive the kingdom of God like a child shall not enter it" (Mark 10:14-15).

Jesus' message became more clear as a result of something else Jesus told the disciples around the same time. They had just completed a long journey from one town to another. Jesus asked them what they had been discussing on the way. They were silent and embarrassed; they had been discussing who was the greatest or most important

among them. Jesus knew this. So he called them around him, and said: "Whoever wants to be first must place himself last of all and be the servant of all" (Mark 9:35 TEV). Jesus took a child and put it before them. "Whoever welcomes in my name one of these children, welcomes me" (Mark 9:37 TEV).

Jesus thus taught that true greatness consists in becoming like a little child, humbly putting oneself into the hands of God, approaching others with the attitude that one is at their service.

Jesus was especially concerned with what he called "stumbling blocks." By that he meant tempting or enticing to sin any of his little ones or those afflicted with weaknesses. Jesus held that we should be prepared to suffer ourselves—he expressed this very strongly by using exaggerated language to say that we should be prepared to cut off our own limbs or organs—rather than allowing others or ourselves to be tempted by sin.

On the subject of pardoning others for what they had done Jesus told a beautiful though sad parable. A servant owed to his master a huge debt,

so big that he could not pay it. But the king took pity on the man, and forgave him his debt, rather than sending him to prison. The servant himself, however, came upon another one of the king's servants who owed him a small debt. The pardoned man treated the other servant harshly and insisted that the debt owed to him be paid in full. When the king heard of this, he exclaimed angrily, "You worthless slave! I forgave you the whole amount you owed me, just because you asked me to. You should have had mercy on your fellow servant, just as I had mercy on you" (Matthew 18:32-33 TEV). And the king had the man thrown into prison.

With this parable, Jesus wanted to teach that it is useless for us to ask God to pardon our sins, if we are not prepared to pardon those who have offended us. However, when we are pardoned by God, God nurtures in our hearts the joy that enables us to pardon others.

27 Prayer was important to Jesus.
He spoke against people
who prayed in public
just to impress other people.
Jesus gave us a model prayer,
called the Lord's Prayer,
or Our Father.

Very often, especially at the end of some long and tiring journey, the disciples of Jesus were accustomed to see him look for some solitary place and then go there to pray, completely absorbed in what he was doing.

Jesus was quite different from some of the other pious people among the Jews; they were accustomed to pray aloud, standing up in the synagogues or even in the public squares, so that all could see and admire them.

Jesus called people of this kind hypocrites, or frauds; they were concerned with how they looked to others, rather than with a real relationship with God.

Finally one day the disciples asked, partly out of curiosity and partly out of true desire to learn, "Lord, teach us to pray" (Luke 11:1). Jesus responded with one of the most beautiful prayers ever prayed, usually called the Lord's Prayer or the Our Father. This has remained the most important Christian prayer ever since.

Here is the prayer as it is recorded in the Gospel of Matthew:

"And in praying do not heap up empty phrases as the Gentiles do; for they think that they will be heard for their many words. Do not be like them, for your Father knows what you need before you ask him. Pray then like this:

Our Father who art in heaven,
Hallowed be thy name.
Thy kingdom come,
Thy will be done,
   On earth as it is in heaven.
Give us this day our daily bread;
And forgive us our debts,
   As we also have forgiven our debtors;
And lead us not into temptation,
   But deliver us from evil.

For if you forgive men their trespasses, your heavenly Father also will forgive you; but if you do not forgive men their trespasses, neither will your Father forgive your trespasses."

(Matthew 6:7-15)

28 According to Jewish law,
the penalty for adultery
was death by stoning.
Enemies of Jesus once brought
an adulterous woman to Jesus.
Jesus said, "Whoever
has committed no sin may throw
the first stone at her."
Her accusers left.
Jesus said to the woman,
"Go, and do not sin again."

The teaching of Jesus was so new and was delivered with such authority that some Pharisees became very hostile toward Jesus. The Pharisees were the group among the Jews who believed themselves to be the true teachers of the Law of God. They accused Jesus of many things. First of all, they criticized him for being concerned about, and even eating with, publicans and sinners. Then they attacked him for considering himself above the Law, as if he had the power to interpret and change it. They were further disturbed because he frequently accused them of hypocrisy. Finally—and this was the worst thing of all—they accused him of claiming to be equal to God or of acting as if he thought he was.

The Pharisees thus were constantly on the lookout for occasions to trap Jesus. They found Jesus to be a threat to law and order as they understood it. One day they believed that they had found a trap that would succeed in discrediting him in the eyes of the people.

It was early in the morning, and, as he usually did when he was in Jerusalem, Jesus went to the Temple, where he taught the people. The scribes and the Pharisees brought to him an adulterous woman who had been caught being unfaithful to her husband.

The Jewish Law was very strict in the punishments it prescribed for sins against the family. Adultery was to be punished by stoning to death. Condemned persons were to be executed by a heavy shower of stones thrown at them. According to the custom, the first stones should be thrown by whoever made the accusation.

The woman was brought before Jesus because his goodness and compassion were known; the enemies of Jesus thought that he might be so bold as to contradict the Law. So they asked Jesus, "Teacher, this woman has been caught in the act of adultery. Now in the Law Moses commanded us to stone such. What do you say about her?" (John 8:4-5).

Jesus was silent. Then he bent down and began to write with his finger on the ground. However, they pressed him for an answer. He looked up and said to them, "Whichever one of you has committed no sin may throw the first stone at her" (John 8:7 TEV).

A silence like that of a tomb fell over the group. One by one the accusers began to go away.

Soon Jesus and the woman alone remained. Jesus got up and said to her kindly, "Woman, where are they? Has no one condemned you?" (John 8:10).

The woman replied that no one had condemned her. Jesus said, "Neither do I condemn you; go, and do not sin again" (John 8:11).

The root of the sin of the Pharisees lay in their pride. They thought that they themselves were "good," and therefore not in need of salvation. Moreover, they despised as sinners or riffraff those whom they considered less good.

Jesus told a special parable about the Pharisees' attitudes. He told how a Pharisee and a publican, or tax collector, went to the Temple to pray at the same time. Many Jews hated the publicans as "public sinners," who had sold themselves to the Romans in return for the job of collecting taxes.

The Pharisee entered the Temple with confidence and stood up to pray. "I thank you, God, that I am not greedy, dishonest, or an adulterer, like everybody else. I thank you that I am not like that tax collector over there. I fast two days a week, and I give you one tenth of all my income" (Luke 18:11-12 TEV).

The publican stood at the back of the Temple. He did not even dare to raise his eyes up to heaven; he merely beat his breast and said, "God, be merciful to me a sinner!" (Luke 18:13).

Jesus told this little story and then said, "I tell you, the tax collector, and not the Pharisee, was in the right with God when he went home. For everyone who makes himself great will be humbled, and everyone who humbles himself will be made great" (Luke 18:14 TEV).

Something like what Jesus recounted in this parable actually happened with Zacchaeus, a chief tax collector in Jericho. By taking advantage of his position, he became rich. One day he learned that Jesus was going to visit Jericho. Zacchaeus was curious to see Jesus, so he joined the crowd in the street. Since he was so short, he climbed into a sycamore tree to get a better view.

When Jesus came into town and approached the tree in which Zacchaeus was perched, Jesus looked up and said, "Hurry down, Zacchaeus, because I must stay in your house today" (Luke 19:5 TEV).

When the other people in the crowd heard this, they were shocked that Jesus was going to be the guest of a public sinner. Zacchaeus, however, was pleased; he had never expected that Jesus would choose to stay at his house. He cordially welcomed Jesus.

And Zacchaeus stood and said to the Lord, "Behold, Lord, the half of my goods I give to the poor; and if I have defrauded any one of anything, I restore it fourfold." And Jesus said to him, "Today salvation has come to this house, since he also is a son of Abraham. For the Son of man came to seek and to save the lost."

(Luke 19:8-10)

29
Jesus often saw the good
in people
that others condemned.
He told a parable
that praised the prayer
of a tax collector.
On another occasion,
Jesus went to the home of
a tax collector
named Zacchaeus.

30

The parable of the prodigal son
is about God's love for us.
It tells about a son
who wastes all his money
and then comes home.
His father welcomes him
with a banquet.
His older brother is jealous.

One of the most famous of all the parables of Jesus is called the parable of the prodigal son. "Prodigal" comes from a Latin word meaning to waste or throw away; in the parable it was applied to a rich young man who caused his own ruin. The two main characters in this parable are the prodigal son himself and his merciful father. The other important character is the older brother. He became extremely jealous at the kind treatment their father gave his younger brother, who had acted so badly; the older brother did not want to celebrate his brother's return. The point is that people cannot truly recognize God as their father if they fail to love their brothers and sisters. A true child of God will suffer with other persons in their loss and rejoice with them in their happiness.

Here is the entire parable in the words of the Gospel of Luke:

"There was a man who had two sons; and the younger of them said to his father, 'Father, give me the share of property that falls to me.' And he divided his living between them. Not many days later, the younger son gathered all he had and took his journey into a far country, and there he squandered his property in loose living. And when he had spent everything, a great famine arose in the country, and he began to be in want. So he went and joined himself to one of the citizens of that country, who sent him into his fields to feed swine. And he would gladly have fed on the pods that the swine ate; and no one gave him anything. But when he came to himself he said, 'How many of my father's hired servants have bread enough and to spare, but I perish here with hunger! I will arise and go to my father, and I will say to him, "Father, I have sinned against heaven and before you; I am no longer worthy to be called your son; treat me as one of your hired servants."' And he arose and came to his father. But while he was yet at a distance, his father saw him and had compassion and ran and embraced him and kissed him. And the son said to him, 'Father, I have sinned against heaven and before you; I am no longer worthy to be called your son.' But the father said to his servants, 'Bring quickly the best robe, and put it on him; and put a ring on his hand, and shoes on his feet; and bring the fatted calf and kill it, and let us eat and make merry; for this my son was dead, and is alive again; he was lost, and is found.' And they began to make merry.

"Now his elder son was in the field; and as he came and drew near to the house, he heard music and dancing. And he called one of the servants and asked what this meant. And he said to him, 'Your brother has come, and your father has killed the fatted calf, because he has received him safe and sound.' But he was angry and refused to go in. His father came out and entreated him, but he answered his father, 'Lo, these many years I have served you, and I never disobeyed your command; yet you never gave me a kid, that I might make merry with my friends. But when this son of yours came, who has devoured your living with harlots, you killed for him the fatted calf!' And he said to him, 'Son, you are always with me, and all that is mine is yours. It was fitting to make merry and be glad, for this your brother was dead, and is alive; he was lost, and is found.'"

(Luke 15:11-32)

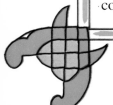

31
The parable
of the good Samaritan
is about being a neighbor.
It tells about an injured man.
He does not get help
from a religious Jew
but from a Samaritan,
a foreigner and heretic.

One day a teacher of the Law asked Jesus what he had to do to be saved. Jesus immediately responded by asking the man what was written in the Law. The man replied, "You shall love the Lord your God with all your heart, and with all your soul, and with all your strength, and with all your mind; and your neighbor as yourself" (Luke 10:27).

But the man was not satisfied when Jesus said that his answer was correct. The man went on to ask, "And who is my neighbor?" (Luke 10:29).

To answer this question, Jesus told one of his best-known parables, the parable of the good Samaritan:

"A man was going down from Jerusalem to Jericho, and he fell among robbers, who stripped him and beat him, and departed, leaving him half dead. Now by chance a priest was going down that road; and when he saw him he passed by on the other side. So likewise a Levite, when he came to the place and saw him, passed by on the other side. But a Samaritan, as he journeyed, came to where he was; and when he saw him, he had compassion, and went to him and bound up his wounds, pouring on oil and wine; then he set him on his own beast and brought him to an inn, and took care of him. And the next day he took out two denarii and gave them to the innkeeper, saying, 'Take care of him; and whatever more you spend, I will repay you when I come back.'" (Luke 10:30-35)

Both the priest and the Levite (the Levites were those who belonged to the tribe of Levi) worked at the Temple; of all persons, they should have been close to God and should have been the first to fulfill the great commandment of love. Yet they apparently did not love the injured man by the roadside. They did not want to get involved; they had other important things to do; they had to get to their destinations.

According to Jesus, these religious men did not fulfill the spirit of the Law. But Jesus went even further. In his story, the one who *did* fulfill the spirit of the law was a Samaritan. The Jews thought of the Samaritans as foreigners and heretics. They had married persons from neighboring nations and were therefore considered an impure race. And they had corrupted the Jewish religion by adding pagan elements and by building another temple. Yet Jesus depicted the Samaritan as helping the injured man and even promising to pay for anything more the man might need.

After telling the parable, Jesus asked the teacher of the Law,

"Which of these three, do you think, proved neighbor to the man who fell among the robbers?" He said, "The one who showed mercy on him." And Jesus said to him, "Go and do likewise." (Luke 10:36-37)

Jesus gave a simple answer to the teacher's question, "Who is my neighbor?" Jesus taught that the important thing is to help anyone in need.

People are attracted to wealth and do everything they can to get it. The problem, though, is deciding what true wealth really is. One kind of wealth comes from money, clothes, land, and other objects that people want. Often this wealth does not last very long. Often it hurts those who have it. There is, however, another kind of wealth. This wealth is found in qualities of the human heart like love, goodness, and truth.

Jesus always was very concerned about the problem of wealth. He wanted his followers to learn to recognize and choose the treasures that do not get used up and worn out, treasures more important than material goods.

Once a rich young man asked Jesus what he had to do to gain eternal life. Jesus reminded him of the need to keep the commandments of God. The rich young man claimed to be observing them. "Teacher, all these I have observed from my youth" (Mark 10:20).

Jesus looked at the young man with love and kindness; he seemed to see in him a desire for true

32 Jesus was concerned about
our finding true wealth.
He was sad when a rich young man
did not want to give up his wealth.
He praised a poor woman
for her generous offering
in the Temple.

wealth. So Jesus told him the truth. "You lack one thing; go, sell what you have, and give to the poor, and you will have treasure in heaven; and come, follow me" (Mark 10:21).

Jesus invited the young man to become one of his own disciples and to choose Jesus himself as his true wealth. The young man hesitated. Then he went away sad, because "he had great possessions" (Mark 10:22) and he was unable to give up these possessions.

Jesus, too, was saddened by the rich young man's choice. He commented to his disciples, "Children, how hard it is to enter the kingdom of God! It is easier for a camel to go through the eye of a needle than for a rich man to enter the kingdom of God" (Mark 10:24-25). The reason for this is that to enter the kingdom of God one must offer one's own heart. That is impossible if a person is trying to obtain the wealth of this world.

On another occasion Jesus applauded a choice totally different from the one made by the rich young man. Jesus was in the Temple watching the people putting money into the Temple offering. Many were pleased when other people noticed them putting in large sums. Then a poor widow approached and put into the box two copper coins, worth a penny. No one paid the slightest attention to her; her gift seemed insignificant. But Jesus noticed.

And he called his disciples to him, and said to them, "Truly, I say to you, this poor widow has put in more than all those who are contributing to the treasury. For they all contributed out of their abundance; but she out of her poverty has put in everything she had, her whole living." (Mark 12:43-44)

By putting her two small coins into the treasury, the poor widow was really offering her whole heart to God.

33 The parable
of the laborers in the vineyard
is about God's generosity.
Some workers worked all day,
some only a hour.
Yet all were paid the same—
not what they had earned
but what was given to them.

For centuries the Chosen People had been taught their
responsibilities toward God. They believed there was a
strong connection between their good works and the
blessings they might expect to receive from God. One
danger of this belief was that some people thought of their
relationship with God merely as a contract, getting something in return for giving something. This was one of the
reasons Jesus told this parable.

One day very early the owner of a vineyard went out
to hire laborers. This was the custom of the time; those
without work assembled in a public place where they could
be hired, even for a few hours, to do seasonal agricultural
work. The owner hired a number of workers and agreed
with them upon the wages they would be paid; then he
put them to work in his vineyard. He went out again about
nine o'clock in the morning and noticed more workers
waiting to be hired. So he sent them to work in his vineyard. However, he did not agree with them on any specific
wages; he merely promised to pay a fair wage. He repeated the same procedure around noon and again at three
in the afternoon. Late in the afternoon the owner found
more laborers standing by doing nothing. He then sent
them to his vineyard too.

At the end of the day, the owner called his foreman and
said, "Call the laborers and pay them their wages, beginning with the last, up to the first" (Matthew 20:8).

Those who had worked only an hour came up and were paid a denarius. As the other workers who had worked longer came up, they too were paid the same amount, a denarius. The workers who had been hired first, who had been working all day, thought they would be paid more than those who had worked less time. But they too were paid only a denarius.

"They took their money and started grumbling against the employer. 'These men who were hired last worked only one hour,' they said, 'while we put up with a whole day's work in the hot sun—yet you paid them the same as you paid us!' 'Listen, friend,' the owner answered one of them, 'I have not cheated you. After all, you agreed to do a day's work for one silver coin. . . . I want to give this man who was hired last as much as I gave you. Don't I have the right to do as I wish with my own money? Or are you jealous because I am generous?'" (Matthew 20:11-15 TEV)

In this parable Jesus was not attempting to teach about social justice or a just wage. He was teaching that we are to be "paid" on the basis of God's generosity, not on the basis of the "rights" that we have earned through our own efforts.

34 One Sabbath Jesus healed
a man who had been born blind.
Jesus' enemies attacked him
for working on the Sabbath.
To Jesus, this was a sign
of their spiritual blindness.

Jesus described himself by saying, "I am the light of the world" (John 8:12). Jesus once performed a miracle on the Sabbath, to show the meaning of these words. He was walking with his disciples in Jerusalem when he saw a young man who had been blind since birth begging from those passing by. Jesus spat on the ground, made some mud with the spit and dirt, and put it on the eyes of the blind man. He told the man to go wash in the pool of Siloam.

The man went and washed himself as directed. When he returned, he could see. By then Jesus had gone. People who knew the blind man well were amazed.

News of this reached the Pharisees, and the man who had been blind from birth was taken to them. In their opinion, Jesus had sinned greatly in "working" on the Sabbath day. Had he not made mud with his saliva? The commandment to "keep holy the Sabbath day" was interpreted very legalistically by the Pharisees. They taught that manual work could not be performed on the Sabbath, even a simple action. Jesus often challenged their strict interpretation.

The Pharisees did not believe that Jesus could have performed such a wonderful miracle. That was impossible.

To the Pharisees it was clear that Jesus *had* broken the rule about the Sabbath; he *was* therefore a sinner. They called back the man who had been healed.

"We know that this man who cured you is a sinner."

"I do not know if he is a sinner or not," the man replied. "One thing I do know: I was blind, and now I see."

"What did he do to you?" they asked. "How did he cure you of your blindness?"

"I have already told you," he answered, "and you would not listen. Why do you want to hear it again? Maybe you, too, would like to be his disciples?"

They insulted him and said, "You are that fellow's disciple; but we are Moses' disciples. We know that God spoke to Moses; as for that fellow, however, we do not even know where he comes from!"

The man answered, "What a strange thing that is! You do not know where he comes from, but he cured me of my blindness! We know that God does not listen to sinners; he does listen to people who respect him and do what he wants them to do. Since the beginning of the world nobody has ever heard of anyone giving sight to a blind person. Unless this man came from God, he would not be able to do a thing."

They answered, "You were born and brought up in sin—and you are trying to teach us?" (John 9:24-34 TEV)

Jesus found the man again and asked him whether he believed in the Son of Man.

The man answered, "Tell me who he is, sir, so that I can believe in him!"

Jesus said to him, "You have already seen him, and he is the one who is talking with you now."

"I believe, Lord!" the man said, and knelt down before Jesus. (John 9:36-38 TEV)

From this the disciples understood that under the influence of Jesus everyone, including the blind, learned to see, whether with the eyes of the body, or, more importantly, the eyes of the heart. Those who refused to be influenced by Jesus, even if their eyes were very good, became blind and fell into darkness.

35 Jesus called himself
the good shepherd.
He loved his friends,
called them by name,
and was ready
to lay down his life
to protect them.

When the prophets of Israel, who had lived before Jesus, wanted to speak about the love and protection lavished on God's people, they used various familiar images. They compared God to a bridegroom, to a gardener, and to a shepherd. The prophets especially used the image of the shepherd to show the need of God's people to be guided, like sheep in a flock.

Jesus also used the image of a shepherd. In the parable of the lost sheep, he spoke of a shepherd with one hundred sheep. When just one went astray, he left the other ninety-nine to go to look for the single one that was lost. When he found the lost sheep, he laid it across his shoulders and brought it back safely. He rejoiced with his friends and neighbors that his lost sheep had been found, as if that one animal had more value than all the others put together (Luke 15:3-7). In this parable Jesus portrayed the concern of God for every single creature.

On another occasion, Jesus described himself as the good shepherd who knew his sheep, who called each one by name, and who led them to abundant pastures. The good shepherd was prepared to lay down his very life for his sheep. In contrast, a paid or hireling shepherd did not really care about the flock.

So Jesus again said to them, "Truly, truly, I say to you, I am the door of the sheep. All who came before me are thieves and robbers; but the sheep did not heed them. I am the door; if any one enters by me, he will be saved, and will go in and out and find pasture. The thief comes only to steal and kill and destroy; I came that they may have life, and have it abundantly. I am the good shepherd. The good shepherd lays down his life for the sheep. He who is a hireling and not a shepherd, whose own the sheep are not, sees the wolf coming and leaves

the sheep and flees; and the wolf snatches them and scatters them. He flees because he is a hireling and cares nothing for the sheep. I am the good shepherd; I know my own and my own know me, as the Father knows me and I know the Father; and I lay down my life for the sheep. And I have other sheep, that are not of this fold; I must bring them also, and they will heed my voice. So there shall be one flock, one shepherd. For this reason the Father loves me, because I lay down my life, that I may take it again. No one takes it from me, but I lay it down of my own accord. I have power to lay it down, and I have power to take it again; this charge I have received from my Father."

(John 10:7-18)

36 A close friend of Jesus,
Lazarus, died suddenly.
Jesus arrived after Lazarus
had been buried.
Jesus raised Lazarus
from the dead and said,
"I am the resurrection
and the life."

In the village of Bethany two sisters, Martha and Mary, lived with their brother, Lazarus. They were very good friends of Jesus. Many times Jesus had enjoyed hospitality at their house. Whenever he came, Martha showed great concern to have everything ready for Jesus.

Her sister, Mary, did not think very much ahead of time about when Jesus was coming. But then when he did arrive, she sat near Jesus and listened to him talking, oblivious to everything else around her. This concentration of Mary's annoyed Martha. One day she even spoke to Jesus about it:

"Lord, don't you care that my sister has left me to do all the work by myself? Tell her to come and help me!" (Luke 10:40 TEV).

The duties of hospitality done by Martha are important, but so is time spent in listening and just being in the presence of Jesus, as Mary chose to do. For Mary it was the better thing to do.

The Lord answered her, "Martha, Martha! You are worried and troubled over so many things, but just one is needed. Mary has chosen the right thing, and it will not be taken away from her." (Luke 10:41-42 TEV)

Sometime later, a great misfortune struck this household. Lazarus suddenly became gravely ill. Jesus was far away. Mary and Martha sent for Jesus immediately, but he took an unusually long time in coming. So Lazarus died and had already been buried for four days when Jesus arrived. Martha went out to meet him. She fell down before him:

Martha said to Jesus, "Lord, if you had been here, my brother would not have died. And even now I know that whatever you ask from God, God will give you." Jesus said to her, "Your brother will rise again." Martha said to him, "I know that he will rise again in the resurrection at the last day." (John 11:21-24)

Martha thought Jesus meant that Lazarus would rise again on the last day, at the end of the world, when all the dead would awaken; only then would she see her loved one. Then Jesus said something quite unexpected:

"I am the resurrection and the life; he who believes in me, though he die, yet shall he live, and whoever lives and believes in me shall never die. Do you believe this?" She said to him, "Yes, Lord; I believe that you are the Christ, the Son of God, he who is coming into the world." (John 11:25-27)

Meanwhile, Lazarus was still dead. Martha went to call Mary, the sister who had listened so intently to Jesus. Mary came to the place where Jesus was, accompanied by many of their mourning friends and relatives. Mary fell down before Jesus and declared that if he had been there, Lazarus would not have died.

Seeing them all weeping, Jesus too was moved. Jesus asked where Lazarus had been buried. They led him there. Then Jesus wept. Some people said, "See how much he loved him!" (John 11:36 TEV). Others wondered whether the man who had healed the blind man could have prevented the death of Lazarus.

Deeply moved once more, Jesus went to the tomb, which was a cave with a stone placed at the entrance. "Take the stone away!" Jesus ordered.

Martha, the dead man's sister, answered, "There will be a bad smell, Lord. He has been buried four days!"

Jesus said to her, "Didn't I tell you that you would see God's glory if you believed?" They took the stone away. Jesus looked up and said, "I thank you, Father, that you listen to me. I know that you always listen to me, but I say this for the sake of the people here, so that they will believe that you sent me." After he had said this, he called out in a loud voice, "Lazarus, come out!" He came out, his hands and feet wrapped in grave cloths, and with a cloth around his face. "Untie him," Jesus told them, "and let him go." (John 11:38-44 TEV)

The crowd was amazed. Jesus had raised from the dead a man who had died several days earlier.

Some of the Pharisees concluded from this incident that Jesus had to be killed. Otherwise everyone would come to believe in him, for the raising of Lazarus was proof of his greatness and power.

37 At the beginning
of Jesus' last week,
he entered Jerusalem
in triumph, riding on a donkey.
The crowds shouted,
"Hosanna to the son of David!"

The time came for Jesus to go up to Jerusalem, a journey that would end with his passion and death. The great prophecies of the Old Testament were being fulfilled.

Centuries earlier, the prophet Zechariah had declared,

"Tell the city of Zion,
Look, your king is coming to you!
He is humble and rides on a donkey
and on a colt, the foal of a donkey."
(Matthew 21:5 TEV)

The description by the prophet meant that the future Messiah would be known for his goodness and his gentleness. But Jesus also decided to act out the prophecy literally. He sent two of his disciples into the city to a place where he said that a donkey with a colt would be tied up. They were to borrow the donkey for his use. Garments were thrown over the donkey, and Jesus mounted. As he rode into Jerusalem, many of the people in the crowd that had gathered along his way threw down their own garments on the road in front of him; others cut palms and branches from trees and spread them in front of Jesus. The crowd sang:

"Hosanna to the Son of David!
Blessed is he who comes in the name of the
    Lord!
Hosanna in the Highest!"   (Matthew 21:9)

The word "Hosanna" originally meant, "save, we pray," but here it is a shout of praise welcoming Jesus as Son of David. "Son of David" was a title used for the Messiah.

So Jesus entered Jerusalem amid all this festivity. A great wave of excitement swept over the city. Those who did not already know him asked who he was. The crowds replied, "This is the prophet Jesus from Nazareth of Galilee" (Matthew 21:11).

The sick and the crippled came up to him, and he healed them. When he arrived at the Temple, the excitement reached its height. The children of Jerusalem were crying out, "Hosanna to the Son of David." When the chief priests and scribes saw all this activity and heard the cries of the children, they were indignant.

They said to him, "Do you hear what these are saying?" And Jesus said to them, "Yes; have you never read,
    'Out of the mouth of babes and sucklings
    thou hast brought perfect praise'?"
                                  (Matthew 21:16)

Jesus was quoting a verse from Psalm 8, an ancient prayer that said God was especially pleased with words of praise from the lips of children. Too many adults remain unable to recognize the grace of God and rejoice in it.

This triumphant reception of Jesus in Jerusalem is still celebrated on Palm Sunday. But it was the last time Jesus would ever experience the applause of the crowd. In fact, this joyous entry into Jerusalem started the very week that would include the betrayal of Jesus and his abandonment by nearly everyone. Before long the same crowds that cried "hosanna" would be crying "crucify him!"

38

The parable
of the marriage feast
is about God's invitation
to all people,
not just a special few.
It tells about a great feast.
Some people who were invited
did not want to come.
So the host invited the poor,
the sick, beggars,
whoever was in the streets.

Among the last parables of Jesus is the parable of the marriage feast. The Hebrew prophets had spoken many times of the marriage feast that God was preparing for his people; the coming of the Messiah or Savior was described as an event like a wedding, full of joy.

But Jesus wanted to warn that this joyous event would not come about except through suffering. So he told the story of a king who had prepared a splendid feast to celebrate the wedding of his son. When the king sent out the invitations, the guests did not want to come. When he heard this, the king could not believe his ears. He sent his servants out again with invitations, but all those invited still reported that they were busy; some had to tend to their own business affairs, others had trips to make, and so on. Nobody could come to the banquet. Some of those who were invited actually insulted and attacked the servants the king had sent out with the invitations.

The king was outraged. He called together his servants and sent them out into the streets and byways to give out invitations to everybody they met, including the poor and the crippled, beggars, and vagabonds. All were to be invited to the marriage feast. Soon the hall was filled to overflowing, and the feast began.

Those who heard this parable when it was first told understood Jesus perfectly: The people who were initially the privileged ones were refusing to be God's friends at the very moment of the great feast prepared for God's people (the incarnation of the Son of God, Jesus Christ). So God was turning to new friends, including the poorest and most miserable people, from among both the Jews and the Gentiles.

Then Jesus added a final touch to the parable. He told how one guest came without a wedding garment; the king therefore ordered him to be cast out of the banquet hall. Jesus meant that even those who answered the general invitation to attend had to do so responsibly. Everyone needed to wear the proper garment for the occasion, that is, to measure up to what was required.

Jesus used a similar parable to show how the best educated and most mature elements of Jewish society were behaving. An owner had rented his vineyard to tenants. When harvest time came, he sent his servants to the tenants to collect his share of the grape harvest. Instead, the tenants beat up his servants and sent them away. The owner therefore decided to send his own son, thinking that surely they would respect him. Instead they beat up the son and murdered him, with the intention of taking over his inheritance.

When they heard about such parables, the scribes and the Pharisees were furious. They realized that Jesus was talking about *them*. Jesus' death was now becoming inevitable.

39 Enemies of Jesus sometimes
asked him hard questions.
They hoped he would say
something illegal or offensive.
For instance, they asked him
whether it was right
to pay taxes.

The Pharisees kept trying to embarrass Jesus. One day they asked him in public if it was lawful to pay taxes and tribute to Caesar, the Roman emperor. This question was a trap because any answer that Jesus might give would displease someone. If Jesus said paying taxes was lawful, then the Pharisees could accuse him of supporting the Roman oppressors. If he said it was not lawful, then he could be denounced to the Roman authorities as a rebel.

Jesus, however, was aware of their evil plan, and so he said, "You hypocrites! Why are you trying to trap me? Show me the coin for paying the tax!"
They brought him the coin, and he asked them, "Whose face and name are these?"
"The Emperor's," they answered.
So Jesus said to them, "Well, then, pay to the Emperor what belongs to the Emperor, and pay to God what belongs to God."
(Matthew 22:18-21 TEV)

The Sadducees were also ready to ridicule the teaching of Jesus. The Pharisees disliked the Sadducees, especially because the latter did not believe in eternal life; but both groups opposed Jesus. The Sadducees were always ready to trip him up. They tried to do it on the subject of the resurrection. Among the Jews at that time there was a law called the law of the levirate. Its purpose was to make families stable and to make sure there were heirs for family goods. According to this law, if a man's brother died without male heirs, the man had to marry his brother's widow. The first son born of this second marriage would then be considered the son of the man who had died without leaving a son.

The Sadducees came before Jesus with a story. A woman had married seven successive brothers, each of whom had died without leaving sons. The Sadducees asked Jesus who, at the time of the resurrection, would be the woman's husband.

Jesus answered them, "How wrong you are! It is because you don't know the Scriptures or God's power. For when the dead rise to life, they will be like the angels in heaven and will not marry." (Matthew 22:29-30 TEV)

Jesus gave a serious answer to a question which the Sadducees had not taken seriously. Jesus said that eternal life was not simply an extension of this earthly life where things such as the continuation of families had to be considered. Rather, eternal life was a kind of life in which all would be united in the love of God.
Jesus went on to answer the Sadducees by quoting back to them the Book of Exodus and pointing out that God was "not God of the dead, but of the living" (Matthew 22:32). Everyone would rise because God would not allow to remain dead those to whom he had promised eternal life.
Sometimes, enemies brought forward these false problems to try to trip up Jesus. At other times, however, people asked very thoughtful questions. Jesus always insisted on one point: The greatest of all the commandments was to love God with all one's might, heart, and soul; and the second most important commandment was to love one's neighbor as oneself. Jesus taught, "On these two commandments depend all the Law and the prophets" (Matthew 22:40).

40 Jesus spoke to his followers about the coming destruction of Jerusalem and the end of the world.

There was one thing the disciples found very hard to understand. How could things just go on as before, after his death and resurrection, which was the central point of all human history?

To answer this perplexing question, Jesus instructed his disciples about the end of the world. Jesus related his teaching on this to his prophecy of the coming destruction of Jerusalem.

And as he came out of the temple, one of his disciples said to him, "Look, Teacher, what wonderful stones and what wonderful buildings!" And Jesus said to him, "Do you see these great buildings? There will not be left here one stone upon another, that will not be thrown down." (Mark 13:1-2)

The disciples were fearful and amazed at this prediction. They asked Jesus when it would happen and what signs would show that the time had come. Jesus had no intention of merely satisfying

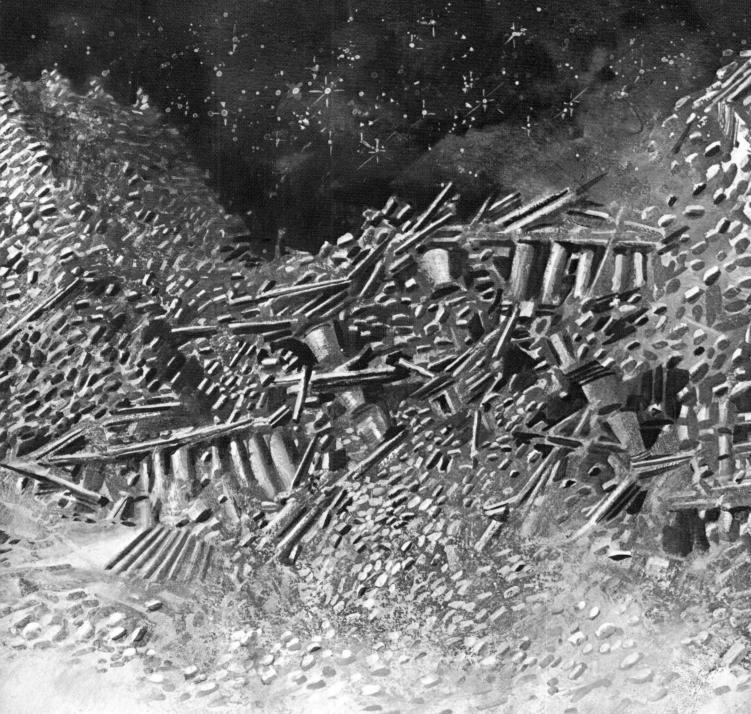

their curiosity. He wanted to sharpen their watch-fulness and to increase their faith.

So he discussed two very different events to-gether. Jesus talked about the coming destruction of Jerusalem. When this occurred, it would mean pain and sorrow for all Jews. Jerusalem was in fact destroyed by the Romans in A.D. 70. But in a mysterious way Jesus linked this catastrophe for the Jews with the catastrophe for all people, the end of the world.

In the course of history there would be wars, revolutions, earthquakes, famines, and other ca-lamities. There would be much suffering. There would especially be suffering for those wishing to remain faithful to the teaching of Jesus. Those things suffered in the name of Jesus, however, would be sufferings charged with hope. They would give meaning to the apparently useless sufferings that human beings inflict on each other and so frequently have to bear without understanding why.

The end of the world will indeed come. Jesus describes it as a catastrophe affecting the whole universe. The Bible says, however, that no one can predict when the end will occur. "Of that day and that hour, no one knows, not even the angels in heaven" (Mark 13:32).

Jesus is telling his disciples that it is important to do the work God asks of them now without expecting permanent results. What will remain are the effects of the love each person shows in doing his or her work.

Jesus himself—according to his own testi-mony—was to return in glory to judge the world and gather in his own.

And then they will see the Son of man coming in clouds with great power and glory. And then he will send out the angels, and gather his elect from the four winds, from the ends of the earth to the ends of heaven. (Mark 13:26-27)

41 The parable of
the wise and foolish young women
is about being ready to meet God.
It tells about two groups waiting
for a wedding feast. One took enough oil
for their lamps; the other group didn't.

Some day we will have to appear before our Lord and judge. Jesus explained this idea once in a beautiful parable. To understand this parable, we have to understand the marriage customs of the ancient Jews. Before the wedding, the unmarried women who were friends of the bride would meet in her house; the unmarried men who were friends of the groom would gather in his house. Each of these groups would spend several days celebrating the coming wedding.

When the day of the wedding arrived, the bridegroom would leave his house, accompanied by his friends; they would all move toward the house of the bride. The bride, accompanied by her friends, would come out to meet the bridegroom. When they met, she would be joyously escorted to her new home, where the marriage feast would then begin.

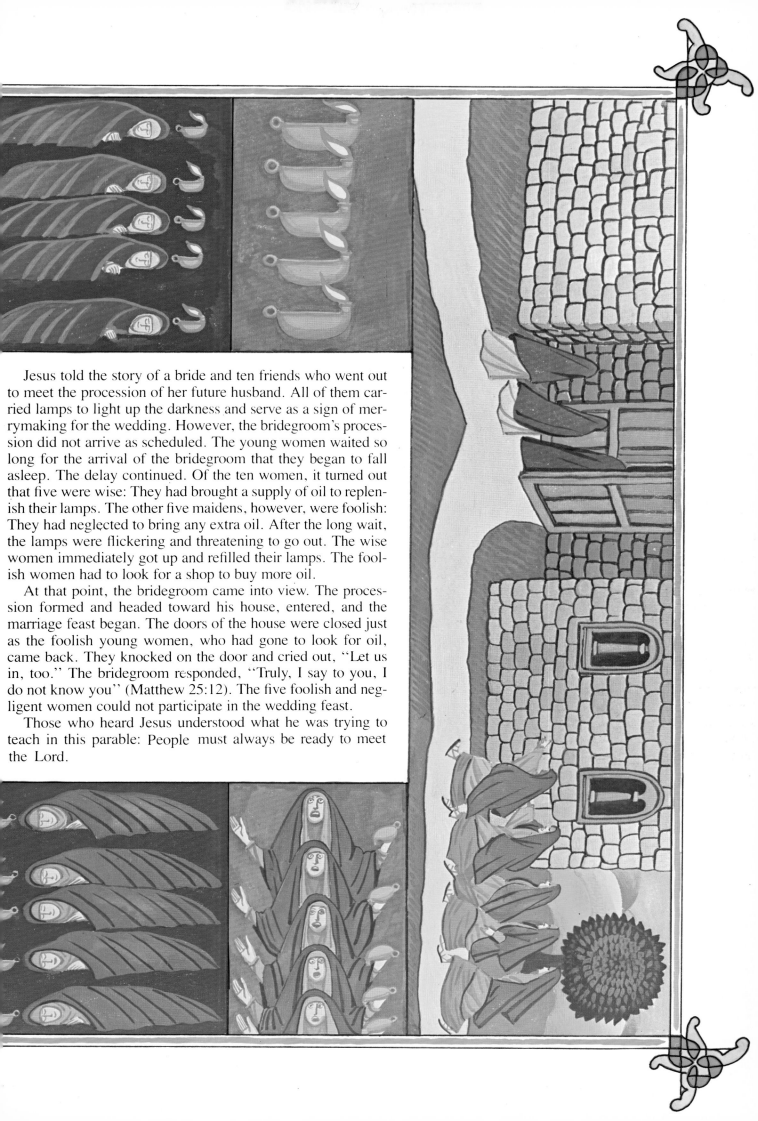

Jesus told the story of a bride and ten friends who went out to meet the procession of her future husband. All of them carried lamps to light up the darkness and serve as a sign of merrymaking for the wedding. However, the bridegroom's procession did not arrive as scheduled. The young women waited so long for the arrival of the bridegroom that they began to fall asleep. The delay continued. Of the ten women, it turned out that five were wise: They had brought a supply of oil to replenish their lamps. The other five maidens, however, were foolish: They had neglected to bring any extra oil. After the long wait, the lamps were flickering and threatening to go out. The wise women immediately got up and refilled their lamps. The foolish women had to look for a shop to buy more oil.

At that point, the bridegroom came into view. The procession formed and headed toward his house, entered, and the marriage feast began. The doors of the house were closed just as the foolish young women, who had gone to look for oil, came back. They knocked on the door and cried out, "Let us in, too." The bridegroom responded, "Truly, I say to you, I do not know you" (Matthew 25:12). The five foolish and negligent women could not participate in the wedding feast.

Those who heard Jesus understood what he was trying to teach in this parable: People must always be ready to meet the Lord.

42 The parable of the last judgment
is about living now
the way God wants us to.
In the parable, persons
are judged by their treatment
of the sick, hungry, and naked.

The centuries in the history of Judea before the coming of Christ were a long period of defeats, disappointments, and oppression. Nevertheless, the Jews remained confident that God would intervene and free them; they were his people. A style of literature called apocalyptical literature grew out of this period of tense expectation. The literature announced a coming cosmic disaster in which evil would be destroyed. The expected disasters were described in various ways, but it was certain that they would bring about a radical change in the human condition. Oppressors would be defeated, and the just would be freed and rule the earth.

Jesus was very well acquainted with this kind of apocalyptic literature. Jesus spoke of the end of the world and of the last judgment, just as the typical apocalyptic literature did. But Jesus described them in terms of the triumphant return of the Messiah.

When Jesus spoke about the end of the world, he emphasized the attitude we should have regarding our end: It can arrive at any moment. We do not know when the end of the world will come, but nevertheless we must be ready for it at any moment.

In the parables about the world's end and the last judgment, however, Jesus taught that this constant watchfulness or vigilance should not require just waiting.

Once again, Jesus was inviting his disciples to learn the true meaning of love. True love is shown in a willingness to serve the poor and needy. Jesus taught that in serving them we are serving him. With the eyes of love true, disciples are able to see Jesus in others. Those without love do not recognize him in the poor and will thereby be excluded from the kingdom of God.

Here are the words of Jesus as reported in the Gospel of Matthew:

"When the Son of man comes in his glory, and all the angels with him, then he will sit on his glorious throne. Before him will be gathered all the nations, and he will separate them one from another as a shepherd separates the sheep from the goats, and he will place the sheep at his right hand, but the goats at the left. Then the King will say to those at his right hand, 'Come, O blessed of my Father, inherit the kingdom prepared for you from the foundation of the world; for I was hungry and you gave me food, I was thirsty and you gave me drink, I was a stranger and you welcomed me, I was naked and you clothed me, I was sick and you visited me, I was in prison and you came to me.' Then the righteous will answer him, 'Lord, when did we see thee hungry and feed thee, or thirsty and give thee drink? And when did we see thee a stranger and welcome thee, or naked and clothe thee? And when did we see thee sick or in prison and visit thee?' And the King will answer them, 'Truly, I say to you, as you did it to one of the least of these my brethren, you did it to me.' Then he will say to those at his left hand, 'Depart from me, you cursed, into the eternal fire prepared for the devil and his angels; for I was hungry and you gave me no food, I was thirsty and you gave me no drink, I was a stranger and you did not welcome me, naked and you did not clothe me, sick and in prison and you did not visit me.' Then they also will answer, 'Lord, when did we see thee hungry or thirsty or a stranger or naked or sick or in prison, and did not minister to thee?' Then he will answer them, 'Truly, I say to you, as you did it not to one of the least of these, you did it not to me.' And they will go away into eternal punishment, but the righteous into eternal life." (Matthew 25:31-46)

In spite of all Jesus' explanations, his disciples were still afraid of the prospect of the life of Jesus coming to an end. Jesus kept referring to his imminent end, and this disturbed them all the more. Sometimes even Jesus himself seemed upset at the idea of what was to come.

He taught unmistakably about his future sacrifice on one occasion when some Greeks said they wished to see him. This teaching looked forward to the acceptance that Jesus' message would later find among the Greeks: People of all nations would be attracted to Jesus but first he must suffer rejection and abandonment.

Jesus compared his own life with a grain of wheat that must first fall into the ground and decompose before producing a new plant stalk with abundant grain.

His disciples did not yet understand this teaching. They were afraid of losing their lives. They did not perceive the good that would come out of this very loss once they had abandoned themselves entirely into God's hands.

This profound story is worth reading in the actual words of the Gospel of John:

Some Greeks were among those who had gone to Jerusalem to worship during the festival. They went to Philip (he was from Bethsaida in Galilee) and said, "Sir, we want to see Jesus."

Philip went and told Andrew, and the two of them went and told Jesus. Jesus answered them, "The hour has now come for the Son of Man to receive great glory. I am telling you the truth: a grain of wheat remains no more than a single grain unless it is dropped into the ground and dies. If it does die, then it produces many grains.

43 The parable
of the grain of wheat
warns that death
has to come before new life.
Jesus was speaking about
his own death and resurrection
and about
the lives of Christians.
The chief priests and Judas
planned ways to get rid of Jesus.

Whoever loves his own life will lose it; whoever hates his own life in this world will keep it for life eternal. Whoever wants to serve me must follow me, so that my servant will be with me where I am. And my Father will honor anyone who serves me.

"Now my heart is troubled—and what shall I say? Shall I say, 'Father, do not let this hour come upon me'? But that is why I came—so that I might go through this hour of suffering. Father, bring glory to your name!"

Then a voice spoke from heaven. "I have brought glory to it, and I will do so again."

The crowd standing there heard the voice, and some of them said it was thunder, while others said, "An angel spoke to him!"

But Jesus said to them, "It was not for my sake that this voice spoke, but for yours. Now is the time for this world to be judged; now the ruler of this world will be overthrown. When I am lifted up from the earth, I will draw everyone to me." (In saying this he indicated the kind of death he was going to suffer.)

The crowd answered, "Our Law tells us that the Messiah will live forever. How, then, can you say that the Son of Man must be lifted up? Who is this Son of Man?"

Jesus answered, "The light will be among you a little longer. Continue on your way while you have the light, so that the darkness will not come upon you; for the one who walks in the dark does not know where he is going. Believe in the light, then, while you have it, so that you will be the people of the light."

(John 12:20-36 TEV)

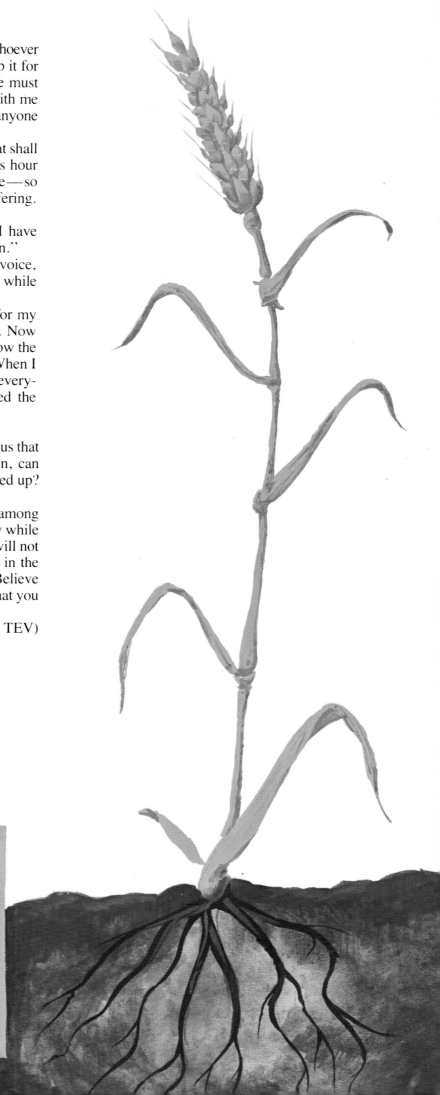

44

At Bethany a woman
anointed Jesus with perfume.
His disciples later saw
that this was like
anointing his body for burial.
Following the orders of Jesus,
his disciples
found an upstairs room
where they could celebrate
the Passover feast.

Several times Jesus had spoken about his coming passion, that is, his suffering. It was now approaching. His enemies were plotting to have him killed. The written narratives of the passion of Jesus are probably the oldest parts of the Gospels of Matthew, Mark, and Luke. Mark begins the description of the events leading to the crucifixion of Jesus with the plot of the chief priests and scribes. The chief priests and scribes met together to seek a way to have Jesus killed secretly. Judas, meanwhile, was preparing to betray his master. In between his account of these two treacherous plans, Mark recorded a gesture of love toward Jesus.

Jesus was at Bethany in the house of Simon the leper, where he had been invited to dinner. A woman approached him with a jar of perfume; she broke the jar and poured the perfume over his head. Her gesture was spontaneous and unplanned. When those present saw what she had done, some of them began to complain loudly. The perfume was very expensive; it could have been sold and the money used to feed the poor. Why had she wasted it in this way? The woman was reproached for her act. But Jesus' reaction was very different.

But Jesus said, "Leave her alone! Why are you bothering her? She has done a fine and beautiful thing for me. You will always have poor people with you, and any time you want to, you can help them. But you will not always have me. She did what she could; she poured perfume on my body to prepare it ahead of time for burial. Now, I assure you that wherever the gospel is preached all over the world, what she has done will be told in memory of her."

(Mark 14:6-9 TEV)

Two things are clear in these words of Jesus: He was thankful to someone who showed kindness to him, and he knew that he soon was going to die. Jesus even connected this anointing by the woman of Bethany with the anointing of bodies before burial, a custom observed at that time.

Right after Jesus referred to his own death, one of his own disciples, Judas Iscariot, decided to provide Jesus' enemies with the opportunity to seize him. Judas went to the chief priests. They received him gladly and offered him money in return for his treachery.

However, Jesus still had time to share with his disciples signs of his great love. The time of the Jewish Passover was near. The disciples awaited his instructions about celebrating it. He sent two of them into the city, where he said they would meet a man carrying a jar of water. They were to follow this man. When the man entered a house, they were to ask the owner of that house to make available a large furnished room where Jesus could celebrate the Passover meal. Following Jesus' orders, the two found the upper room where Jesus would celebrate with his disciples and leave with them for all time the great sign of his love, the Eucharist.

45 At their last meal together
Jesus and his friends
celebrated the Passover.
They remembered the exodus
from slavery in Egypt.
At the meal Jesus
instituted the Eucharist
to celebrate
his sacrificial death.

The festive upper room was prepared for celebrating the Passover, a meal with a very long history. At first the meal was a rite of shepherds and herdsmen. Before setting out in the spring to find suitable pastures for their flocks, they sacrificed one of the young animals as an offering or petition to ensure fertility and the protection of the entire flock. From these beginnings arose the practice of eating a lamb roasted over the fire with unleavened bread and bitter herbs.

Then people began to celebrate this shepherd's rite when commemorating the liberation of Israel from Egypt under Moses. Little by little the memory of this liberation from slavery in Egypt came to be the principal meaning of the rite. The old shepherd's observance took on a new and richer meaning. It came to commemorate the night in which the Lord had struck down the firstborn of the Egyptians while passing over the houses of the Israelites. It also commemorated the passage through the Red Sea when the Israelites emerged unharmed from the dangerous waters.

However, the rite was not merely a commemoration of these past events. When they celebrated the Passover, Jews believed they were actually reenacting the events of their liberation. They believed they were once again actively involved in being freed from oppression. They were once again passing unharmed through the raging waters of history.

The Jewish Passover thus had many centuries of tradition behind it, and its celebration followed an exactly fixed and regular pattern, whether it

was celebrated among a family or in the Temple. Within a family, the father or other head of the family blessed the bread and wine and explained the meaning of what was taking place. Within a religious community, the rabbi or teacher presided.

In the upper room at the time of the Last Supper, as Christians have come to call it, Jesus and his disciples were following a fixed and familiar ritual. However, the teacher of Nazareth introduced some totally new and startling words.

While they were eating, Jesus took a piece of bread, gave a prayer of thanks, broke it, and gave it to his disciples. "Take it," he said, "this is my body."

Then he took a cup, gave thanks to God, and handed it to them; and they all drank from it. Jesus said, "This is my blood, which is poured out for many, my blood which seals God's covenant. I tell you, I will never again drink this wine until the day I drink the new wine in the Kingdom of God." (Mark 14:22-25 TEV)

These strange new words surprised the disciples. Jesus was no longer inviting them to celebrate the liberation of Israel from slavery in Egypt.

Instead he was inviting them to share in a new Covenant of his own blood to be poured out in the course of his own sacrifice and death. Unmistakably the broken bread and the wine poured out during the meal related to his sacrifice on the cross.

This rite was no longer to celebrate the liberation from slavery in Egypt. It was, rather, to celebrate the sacrifice of Jesus himself, who freely gave up his own life for all!

Mark's story of the institution of the Eucharist emphasized that it was a free gift from God, in no way deserved by the disciples—or by the human race as a whole.

Jesus had already been betrayed at the very moment when he gave a wholly new meaning to the ancient Passover sacrifice-meal. He gave to it the meaning of his own sacrifice. Christians were to call it "Eucharist," or "thanksgiving." But the celebration of the Eucharist is not merely a commemoration of the sacrificing death of the Lord; it is also a sign of the risen Christ present in the community of believers whenever the Eucharist or Holy Communion is celebrated.

46 After supper Jesus washed
the feet of his disciples,
a sign that they were to be
servants of others, as Jesus was.
Jesus then warned them that
one of them would betray him
and one would deny
knowing him.

The Last Supper was a special moment, a solemn occasion when Jesus opened his heart and allowed his deepest love to be seen more clearly. After they had all eaten, Jesus arose from the table, laid aside his outer garments, and fashioned a sort of apron which he tied around his waist. Then Jesus picked up a basin, filled it with water, and began to wash and dry the feet of his disciples. They were dumbfounded since this action was one of complete humility. Peter did not want to allow Jesus to serve him in this way since Peter believed he should be the one acting as servant.

(Jesus) came to Simon Peter, who said to him, "Are you going to wash my feet, Lord?"

Jesus answered him, "You do not understand now what I am doing, but you will understand later."

Peter declared, "Never at any time will you wash my feet!"

"If I do not wash your feet," Jesus answered, "you will no longer be my disciple."

Simon Peter answered, "Lord, do not wash only my feet, then! Wash my hands and head, too!" (John 13:6-9 TEV)

What Jesus did was not merely an act of humility. It was also a symbol of the divine plan of salvation through Jesus' giving of himself for humanity. Peter's objections here, only a few hours before Jesus' death, were the same as those he had spoken earlier when Jesus first told his disciples that the Son of Man would have to suffer. Peter had protested when Jesus talked about his own suffering and death. On that earlier occasion, Jesus' reaction had been very severe: "Get behind me, Satan! . . . You are not on the side of God, but of men" (Matthew 16:23). Now this same scene was repeated in the upper room. To be a follower of Jesus required a different scale of values from those conventionally accepted in human society:

"You call me Teacher and Lord, and it is right that you do so, because that is what I am. I, your Lord and Teacher, have just washed your feet. You, then, should wash one another's feet. I have set an example for you, so that you will do just what I have done for you. I am telling you the truth: no slave is greater than his master, and no messenger is greater than the one who sent him. Now that you know this truth, how happy you will be if you put it into practice!" (John 13:13-17 TEV)

Service to others as the expression of the love of Jesus was to become the fundamental law of the new kingdom Jesus was founding. So Peter and the other disciples, called to lead that new community, had to be the first to understand and apply this new law of love.

Jesus did something else at the Last Supper that allowed the disciples to see the depths of his heart. He predicted his own betrayal. "Truly, truly, I say to you, one of you will betray me" (John 13:21).

The disciples were dismayed by this prediction. To John, Jesus revealed the name of the traitor, Judas. None of this relieved the suffering of Jesus, however; Jesus felt completely alone. The disciples could not understand what was happening; Peter, for example, made bold declarations of how he would stand by Jesus.

Jesus had to say to him, sadly, "Truly, I say to you, this very night, before the cock crows, you will deny me three times" (Matthew 26:34).

The Last Supper had begun as a celebration of the Passover meal. It ended on a sorrowful note with Jesus looking toward what was to come and the disciples feeling perplexed and afraid.

47

Jesus had much to say
to his disciples after supper.
He spoke of their relationship
with him and said,
"I am the vine;
you are the branches."
He promised to be with them
forever in spirit.

Following the familiar ritual, after the Passover
meal Jesus and the disciples chanted Psalms 113
through 118. The Jews recited these songs of praise
to God at the end of their Passover banquet. Almost as if he wished to get away from the sadness
of the moment, Jesus then invited the disciples to
leave the upper room with him and head for the
Garden of Gethsemane.

Between leaving the upper room after the Passover meal and arriving in the garden, Jesus spoke
for a long time to the disciples, according to John's
narrative. Perhaps Jesus continued to talk after they
left the upper room; perhaps he spoke on the ter-
race of the house or during their journey. Very
possibly, John added to Jesus' words here teachings Jesus had given to the apostles at other times
and places. Whatever their origin, John's gospel
includes no less than four chapters here known as
the "farewell discourse." In these chapters, the
evangelist gives a beautiful, poetic summary of
the teaching of Jesus.

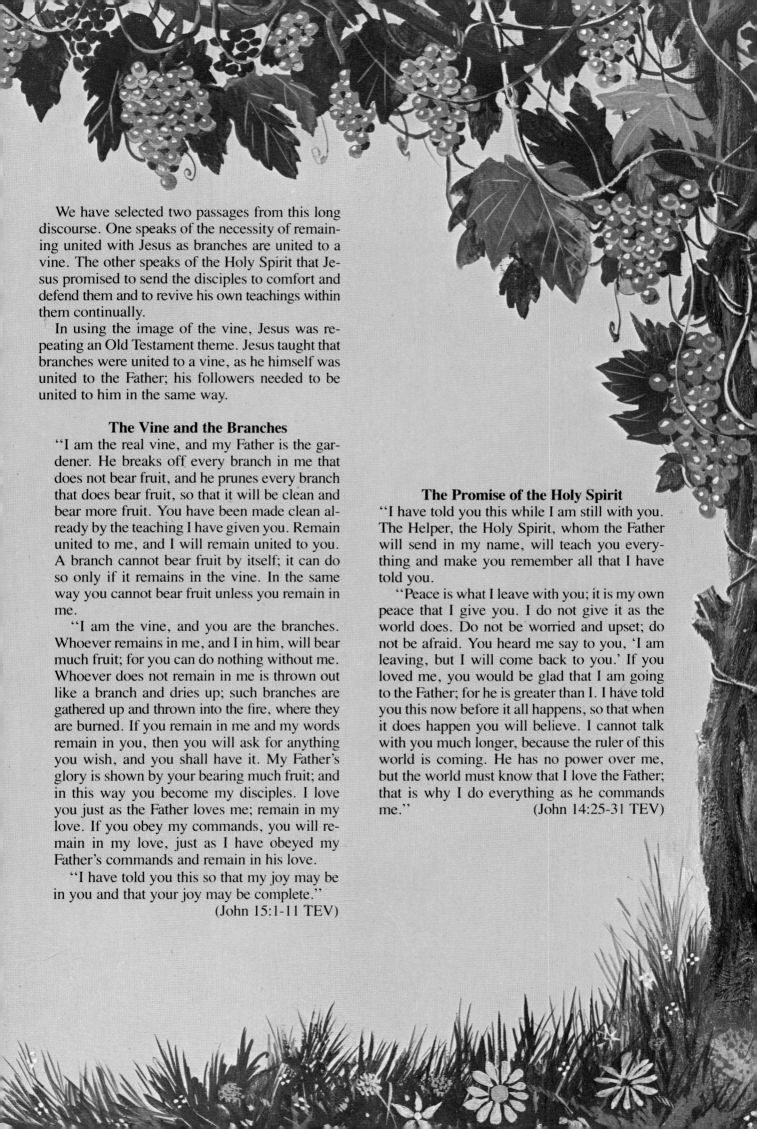

We have selected two passages from this long discourse. One speaks of the necessity of remaining united with Jesus as branches are united to a vine. The other speaks of the Holy Spirit that Jesus promised to send the disciples to comfort and defend them and to revive his own teachings within them continually.

In using the image of the vine, Jesus was repeating an Old Testament theme. Jesus taught that branches were united to a vine, as he himself was united to the Father; his followers needed to be united to him in the same way.

The Vine and the Branches

"I am the real vine, and my Father is the gardener. He breaks off every branch in me that does not bear fruit, and he prunes every branch that does bear fruit, so that it will be clean and bear more fruit. You have been made clean already by the teaching I have given you. Remain united to me, and I will remain united to you. A branch cannot bear fruit by itself; it can do so only if it remains in the vine. In the same way you cannot bear fruit unless you remain in me.

"I am the vine, and you are the branches. Whoever remains in me, and I in him, will bear much fruit; for you can do nothing without me. Whoever does not remain in me is thrown out like a branch and dries up; such branches are gathered up and thrown into the fire, where they are burned. If you remain in me and my words remain in you, then you will ask for anything you wish, and you shall have it. My Father's glory is shown by your bearing much fruit; and in this way you become my disciples. I love you just as the Father loves me; remain in my love. If you obey my commands, you will remain in my love, just as I have obeyed my Father's commands and remain in his love.

"I have told you this so that my joy may be in you and that your joy may be complete."

(John 15:1-11 TEV)

The Promise of the Holy Spirit

"I have told you this while I am still with you. The Helper, the Holy Spirit, whom the Father will send in my name, will teach you everything and make you remember all that I have told you.

"Peace is what I leave with you; it is my own peace that I give you. I do not give it as the world does. Do not be worried and upset; do not be afraid. You heard me say to you, 'I am leaving, but I will come back to you.' If you loved me, you would be glad that I am going to the Father; for he is greater than I. I have told you this now before it all happens, so that when it does happen you will believe. I cannot talk with you much longer, because the ruler of this world is coming. He has no power over me, but the world must know that I love the Father; that is why I do everything as he commands me."

(John 14:25-31 TEV)

48 Jesus prayed for his disciples and for those who would become disciples through their teaching.

One chapter from the farewell discourse to his disciples—the ones closest to him who would be known as apostles—contains the prayer of Jesus for them and for all who would also become disciples through them.

After Jesus finished saying this, he looked up to heaven and said, "Father, the hour has come. Give glory to your Son, so that the Son may give glory to you. For you gave him authority over all mankind, so that he might give eternal life to all those you gave him. And eternal life means to know you, the only true God, and to know Jesus Christ, whom you sent. I have shown your glory on earth; I have finished the work you gave me to do. Father! Give me glory in your presence now, the same glory I had with you before the world was made.

"I have made you known to those you gave me out of the world. They belonged to you, and you gave them to me. They have obeyed your word, and now they know that everything you gave me comes from you. I gave them the message that you gave me, and they received it; they know that it is true that I came from you, and they believe that you sent me.

"I pray for them. I do not pray for the world but for those you gave me, for they belong to you. All I have is yours, and all you have is mine; and my glory is shown through them. And now I am coming to you; I am no longer in the world, but they are in the world. Holy Father! Keep them safe by the power of your name, the name you gave me, so that they may be one just as you and I are one. While I was with them, I kept them safe by the power of your name, the name you gave me. I protected them, and not one of them was lost, except the

man who was bound to be lost—so that the scripture might come true. And now I am coming to you, and I say these things in the world so that they might have my joy in their hearts in all its fullness. I gave them your message, and the world hated them, because they do not belong to the world, just as I do not belong to the world. I do not ask you to take them out of the world, but I do ask you to keep them safe from the Evil One. Just as I do not belong to the world, they do not belong to the world. Dedicate them to yourself by means of the truth; your word is truth. I sent them into the world, just as you sent me into the world. And for their sake I dedicate myself to you, in order that they, too, may be truly dedicated to you.

"I pray not only for them, but also for those who believe in me because of their message. I pray that they may all be one. Father! May they be in us, just as you are in me and I am in you. May they be one, so that the world will believe that you sent me. I gave them the same glory you gave me, so that they may be one, just as you and I are one: I in them and you in me, so that they may be completely one, in order that the world may know that you sent me and that you love them as you love me.

"Father! You have given them to me, and I want them to be with me where I am, so that they may see my glory, the glory you gave me; for you loved me before the world was made. Righteous Father! The world does not know you, but I know you, and these know that you sent me. I made you known to them, and I will continue to do so, in order that the love you have for me may be in them, and so that I also may be in them." (John 17:1-26 TEV)

49 Jesus and his disciples
went to pray
in the garden of Gethsemane.
Jesus needed strength
to face the day ahead.
Despite his despair,
he prayed to his father,
"Your will be done."
His disciples fell asleep.
Jesus was arrested
in Gethsemane.

After they left the upper room where they had eaten the Last Supper, Jesus and the apostles went toward the garden of Gethsemane. *Gethsemane* was a Hebrew word for the press used to crush the olives that were harvested for oil. The garden, or orchard, was located in the Kidron valley at the foot of the Mount of Olives. Jesus and the apostles knew this place well, for they had been there many times.

This time things were different. The teacher was unable to shake off his sorrow and sadness. Jesus went off away from them to pray. He had done this many times before, but this time not even prayer was able to lessen his anguish. He went back to get Peter, James, and John, the apostles who had glimpsed his glory on Mount Tabor; he asked that they stay awake and wait with him.

No matter how hard they tried, however, the three apostles were unable to stay awake. Jesus

was left alone with his sorrow, apparently abandoned even by God.

It seemed that Jesus was utterly defeated, overwhelmed by sorrow and by the thought of death, by his betrayal and abandonment by his own apostles, and by the apparent indifference of the Father. Nevertheless he continued to pray, to ask the Father for help. "*Abba*, Father, all things are possible for thee; remove this cup from me; yet not what I will but what thou wilt" (Mark 14:36). At the very moment when Jesus seemed to be most abandoned, he called upon the Father with even greater confidence than ever before, using the familiar name that small children use to address their fathers. *Abba* is more accurately translated as "daddy" than as "father."

Like a small child with confidence in his father, Jesus declared, "Father, you know better than I what is good for me and good for everyone in the world. I'm afraid of what's ahead for me, but I nevertheless will do what you want, even if it causes me the greatest suffering."

Jesus passed the test of humility and suffering; he overcame the temptation to try to escape what lay ahead. He rose up from where he had fallen, awakened the apostles, and resolutely went forward to face his suffering and death.

At that point, Judas appeared with a crowd, including armed men. Judas greeted his teacher with a kiss. At this signal from Judas, the armed men crowded around Jesus and arrested him. Once again, Peter demonstrated how rash and impetuous he was. He grabbed a sword and cut off the ear of a servant of the high priest. Jesus offered no resistance himself and immediately ordered Peter to put away the sword. (According to Luke, Jesus healed the ear of the unfortunate servant who had gotten in Peter's way.)

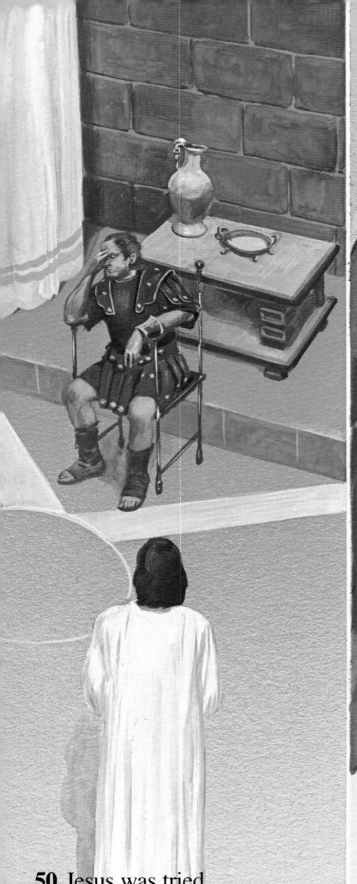

50 Jesus was tried
by the Jewish Sanhedrin
and by Pontius Pilate,
the Roman governor.
He was condemned to death.
The soldiers mocked him.
As Jesus had said, Peter
denied that he knew Jesus.

Those who had arrested Jesus in the garden brought him before their chiefs, the members of the Sanhedrin. This council usually met in a room next to the Temple. However, owing to the lateness of the hour, this time they were assembled in the house of Caiaphas, the high priest.

Any charge was supposed to specify what the defendant was accused of, but the numerous witnesses against Jesus did not succeed in establishing any real charge; indeed, they contradicted each other on various points. At that point, the high priest rose up, and formally interrogated Jesus, "Are you the Christ, the Son of the Blessed?" (Mark 14:61).

Up to that point Jesus had not said a word. But now he was facing the highest political authority among his own people. He replied boldly, "I am; and you will see the Son of man sitting at the right

hand of Power, and coming with the clouds of heaven'' (Mark 14:62).

This reply may sound a bit strange to our ears. To the Jews who heard Jesus say it, however, his meaning was plain. Jesus was referring to two famous Old Testament prophecies and clearly claiming to be the Messiah. The high priest cried out, ''Why do we still need witnesses? You have heard his blasphemy. What is your decision?'' (Mark 14:63-64).

The people responded in chorus, agreeing that Jesus was guilty of blasphemy. Blasphemy meant reviling the name of God or openly claiming to be a messiah.

What were the disciples doing all this time? Where were they? They had left Jesus alone during his agony in the garden. Now they had deserted him and fled. Only Peter had followed, and he followed from a distance. He was below in the courtyard of the high priest's house, trying to find out what was happening. One of the maids in the high priest's house approached him and asked him whether he was one of those who had been with Jesus. Taken by surprise, Peter denied it and moved outside. Again the maid saw him and insisted that he was one of Jesus' men. Peter once again denied knowing Jesus. Other servants accused him later on, pointing out that he, too, was a Galilean. For the third time Peter denied knowing Jesus.

Jesus' prophecy had come true. A cock crowed, and Peter remembered what Jesus had predicted. Peter broke down and wept.

Jesus was tied and taken before the Roman governor, the procurator of Judea, Pontius Pilate. Pilate asked him, ''Are you the King of the Jews?'' And he answered him, ''You have said so.'' And the chief priests accused him of many things. And Pilate again asked him, ''Have you no answer to make? See how many charges they bring against you.'' But Jesus made no further answer, so that Pilate wondered.

(Mark 15: 2-5)

Pilate then made a feeble attempt to save this silent and mysterious Galilean. The Roman governors had for some years shown mercy by each year releasing a prisoner during the Passover season. Pilate decided to make use of this custom. He asked the crowd, ''Do you want me to release for you the King of the Jews?'' (Mark 15:9)

The chief priests stirred up the crowd to call for the release of another prisoner, Barabbas, who had committed murder. Mark recorded this fact to point out that the crowd preferred even a murderer to Jesus. When Pilate asked what should be done with Jesus, the crowd cried out, ''Crucify him!'' (Mark 15:13 TEV).

Then Jesus was subjected to cruel mockery, as was the custom among these soldiers at a frontier garrison. They pretended to pay him royal honors. They dressed him in a purple mantle or cloak. They plaited a crown of thorns and placed it on his head. They pretended to kneel down before him, kiss his hand, and pay homage to him. ''Hail, King of the Jews!'' they cried (Mark 15:18). They struck and slapped him and spat on him. It was a cruel kind of joke. Jesus was utterly alone.

51 Jesus was led to Calvary,
a hill near Jerusalem,
to be crucified.
The sign over his head said,
"Jesus of Nazareth,
King of the Jews."

It had now been twelve or thirteen hours since Jesus' arrest. Between Thursday night, when he was arrested, and Friday morning he had undergone two official "trials" or judgments and one private one in the house of Caiaphas. He had been mocked, struck, slapped, and spat upon. He had been condemned to death by the representatives of the Sanhedrin, and this condemnation had been ratified by the Roman governor.

The events of the long night had followed one another rapidly—some scholars claim too rapidly—because the chief priests and scribes wanted to see Jesus condemned before the height of the Passover celebrations. The evangelists were more eager to record the religious meaning of Christ's saving death than to give a complete account of everything that took place.

Events moved even more swiftly after the condemnation of Jesus. The only interruption was the cruel game the Roman soldiers played with Jesus in pretending to accord him royal honors. Even this game, however, must not have lasted very long. When the game was over, Jesus was dressed again in his own garments, and the procession began moving towards the place where Jesus was to be crucified. This procession consisted of Jesus, two thieves who were condemned to death, the Roman soldiers escorting them, and a throng of onlookers, among whom were perhaps a few relatives or disciples of Jesus.

Jesus and the two other condemned men were carrying the crosspiece of what would be their crosses. They were headed towards the hill of Calvary, a height near the gate of Jerusalem and around 600 yards from the residence of the Roman governor. The distance was not great, but nevertheless it was agony for the condemned men to walk it, given the physical conditions to which they had been reduced. This was particularly true in Jesus' case. Although he is represented in the gospels as being unusually strong and healthy, Jesus seemed to be absolutely worn out and unable to go even half the distance carrying his heavy load.

The soldiers were in a hurry, and they were in no mood to be patient with delays on the road. At a certain point the procession encountered a man named Simon, from the African city of Cyrene. The soldiers pressed him into service and made him carry the heavy crosspiece that one of their prisoners no longer seemed able to carry by himself.

Among those who followed the condemned man were certain women of Jerusalem. They were sincerely grieved by what was taking place. At a certain point Jesus turned to them and said: "Daughters of Jerusalem, do not weep for me, but weep for yourselves and for your children" (Luke 23:28). In this encounter with the sympathetic women, the evangelist Luke portrays Jesus as a person who seeks to comfort others rather than to be comforted by them. The words of Jesus mean "weep not so much for me as for yourselves and your children."

Meanwhile the procession arrived at the hill of Calvary. It was nearly noon. The prisoners were stretched out on the ground. Then their hands were nailed to the heavy crosspieces they had been carrying. These bars were then fastened to poles already planted upright in the ground. This was the way execution by crucifixion was carried out.

Above the head of each crucified prisoner a brief announcement stated the reasons for his condemnation. Above the head of Jesus, the sign read, "Jesus of Nazareth, King of the Jews."

This inscription was a bit of revenge taken by Pilate against the Jewish leaders. According to the evangelists, this was written in three languages, Hebrew, Greek, and Latin. So it was something of a message for the whole world, written in the common spoken languages of the period.

At the foot of the cross, people were still unable to understand the significance of what was happening. Up to the end, many still expressed their scorn and contempt towards Jesus.

And those who passed by derided him, wagging their heads, and saying, "Aha! You who would destroy the temple and build it in three days, save yourself, and come down from the cross!" So also the chief priests mocked him to one another with the scribes, saying, "He saved others; he cannot save himself. Let the Christ, the King of Israel, come down now from the cross, that we may see and believe." Those who were crucified with him also reviled him.
(Mark 15:29-32)

Once again, words intended to make fun of Jesus contained great truths in them. Jesus *had* saved others while refusing to spare himself. The crucifixion seemed violent and absurd; still it was being used for God's purposes. Jesus himself had taught that the grain of wheat would not bear fruit without dying first.

52 Even on the cross, Jesus
showed concern for others:
a thief dying on a cross
next to his,
and his mother Mary.

Up to now we have followed primarily the Gospel of Mark in telling the story of the passion of Christ—his suffering and death. Mark seemed to emphasize the solitude of Jesus. Some stories in the other gospels indicate that Jesus was not left entirely alone on the cross.

One episode recounted by Luke tells how the two thieves who were crucified with Jesus reacted to him. One of them expressed scorn and contempt. The other thief, however, told the first one he ought to be ashamed of himself. They were both going to die soon, and they ought to be preparing to meet their Maker. The two thieves, at least, were suffering for what they had done, while Jesus was truly innocent. Then this second thief turned to Jesus.

And he said, "Jesus, remember me when you come into your kingdom." And he said to him, "Truly, I say to you, today you will be with me in Paradise." (Luke 23:42-43)

When he died on the cross between two thieves, Jesus was not helped by those he had helped. The crowds who had flocked to listen to him abandoned him in his hour of danger. Only a very few of his followers went with him as far as Calvary. This small group included his mother Mary and John, the first of his apostles to recover from the shock of his arrest and try to return to him. Jesus could see them from where he hung on the cross.

When Jesus saw his mother, and the disciple whom he loved standing near, he said to his mother, "Woman, behold, your son!" Then he said to the disciple, "Behold, your mother!" And from that hour the disciple took her to his own home. (John 19:26-27)

Even while he was on the cross, Jesus still thought of others before himself.

But the end was near. The weather took a turn for the worse; dark clouds covered the sky, and it became almost as dark as night. At about three in the afternoon Jesus cried out in the words of the psalm, "My God, my God, why hast thou forsaken me?" (Mark 15:34). Someone held up to Jesus a sponge soaked in vinegar wine often used to quench thirst. Jesus uttered a loud cry and breathed his last.

Jesus' death shows us the love of God for humanity. God allowed even one close to himself to die a painful death for the benefit of others. Yet Jesus did not die like a puppet with God pulling the strings. He willingly gave himself for the salvation of humanity.

Better than any words we ourselves might devise, however, the words of Scripture can help us think about and understand the meaning of the violent death of Jesus:

The Hope of the Just Is Full
of Immortality

But the souls of the righteous are in the hand
    of God,
and no torment will ever touch them.
In the eyes of the foolish they seemed to have
    died,
and their departure was thought to be an
    affliction,
and their going from us to be their destruction;
but they are at peace.
For though in the sight of men they were
    punished,
their hope is full of immortality.
Having been disciplined a little, they will
    receive great good,
because God tested them and found them
    worthy of himself;
like gold in the furnace he tried them,
and like a sacrificial burnt offering he
    accepted them.
In the time of their visitation they will shine
    forth,
and will run like sparks through the stubble.
They will govern nations and rule over
    peoples,
and the Lord will reign over them for ever.

                         (Wisdom 3:1-8)

He Humbled Himself and Became
Obedient unto Death

He always had the nature of God,
    but he did not think that by force he should
    try to become equal with God.
Instead of this, of his own free will he gave
    up all he had,
and took the nature of a servant.
He became like man
    and appeared in human likeness.
He was humble and walked the path of
    obedience all the way to death—his death
    on the cross.
For this reason God raised him to the highest
    place above
and gave him the name that is greater than
    any other name.
And so, in honor of the name of Jesus
    all beings in heaven, on earth, and in the
    world below
    will fall on their knees,
and all will openly proclaim that Jesus Christ
    is Lord
to the glory of God the Father.

              (Philippians 2:5-11 TEV)

53 Jesus was taken down
from the cross
soon after he died.
Joseph of Arimathea
provided a tomb.
Jesus was buried,
and a large stone was rolled
in front of the tomb.

The same haste shown in the judgment and execution of Jesus marked the events that took place right after his death. It was already after three in the afternoon on Friday; that same evening the Sabbath would begin. The change of days for the Jews did not take place at midnight but rather in the evening, at sunset. On the Sabbath day, especially the Sabbath of the Passover week, Jews were forbidden to touch the dead. Therefore, little time remained in which to act if the body of Jesus were not to remain hanging on the cross for the next couple of days. Quick action had to be taken. Jesus' followers, as well as those responsible for his death, agreed on this point. The chief priests and scribes wanted the evidence of their injustice and cruelty removed, and the disciples did not want Jesus' body exposed before the crowds who would throng the city on the following day.

Once again it was for Pilate to decide. The chief priests asked that the executions be completed quickly. Pilate sent soldiers to finish the job. They broke the legs of the two thieves, but when they arrived at the cross of Jesus, they hesitated. He seemed to be dead already. To confirm this, one of the soldiers pierced his side with a spear.

The evangelist John thought it of great importance that no bone in Jesus' body was broken.

John remembered the custom of sacrificing the paschal lamb (which was carried out at the same hour that Jesus was crucified). The sacrificial lamb had to be intact, with no broken bones. When the bones of Jesus were also left unbroken, it reminded the evangelist that Jesus was the true Lamb of God, the true pashcal sacrifice.

When Jesus' side was pierced with the Roman soldier's spear, blood and water flowed from the wound. The blood and water were symbols of the Eucharist and baptism, the central sacraments of the Church.

The chief priests and scribes had moved to have the bodies removed before the Sabbath. Disciples of Jesus also moved rapidly. Among the disciples involved there was Joseph of Arimathea, a member of the same Sanhedrin that had condemned Jesus to death. The fact that such a man was a disciple of Jesus indicates that those attracted to Jesus and his teaching were not only fishermen and housewives from Galilee. Even some influential people from the upper classes had become followers of Jesus.

Joseph of Arimathea was allowed to see Pilate, from whom he requested permission to take care of Jesus' body. Generally the Romans allowed the families or friends to take the bodies of those who

had been executed. Pilate, however, was perplexed in this case. Extraordinary things had been expected of Jesus, a very unusual Jew. Pilate could scarcely believe that Jesus had been finished off so quickly and easily. He summoned a centurion and asked for a confirmation of the fact that Jesus was dead. When this was confirmed, Pilate gave permission to Joseph of Arimathea to dispose of Jesus' body.

Joseph went back to Calvary along with several other disciples. They removed the nails, took Jesus' body down from the cross, wrapped it in a shroud, and took it away for burial. The journey was not long. Not far away was a burial tomb of the family of Joseph of Arimathea, and they buried Jesus there.

The tomb in which Jesus was laid resembled the tombs common among the wealthier people of Palestinian Jewish society. It was hollowed out of solid rock. Another large stone covered the entrance; this had to be rolled aside. Inside was a small entrance way leading to a burial room; inside that, on a kind of stone bench, Jesus was laid. The disciples would have liked to honor his body, but there was little time. The stone was rolled back over the entrance, and Jesus was buried.

54 Two days later, friends of Jesus
went to the tomb. They found it empty.
Jesus appeared to his disciples, both men and women.

"Men of Israel, hear these words: Jesus of Nazareth, a man attested to you by God with mighty works and wonders and signs which God did through him in your midst, as you yourselves know—this Jesus, delivered up according to the definite plan and foreknowledge of God, you crucified and killed by the hands of lawless men. But God raised him up, having loosed the pangs of death, because it was not possible for him to be held by it. . . . Let all the house of Israel therefore know assuredly that God has made him both Lord and Christ, this Jesus whom you crucified."

(Acts 2:22-24,36)

In these words the apostle Peter, the leader of the small community of Jesus' disciples, first preached the good news of salvation in Jesus through his death on the cross and his resurrection to new life.

On the Sabbath that followed the crucifixion, Jesus' disciples kept the Sabbath day of rest, as was their custom. Naturally, they could think of little except the violent events of the day before. In particular, the women among the disciples of Jesus wanted to do the accustomed funeral honors to the body of Jesus. According to Jewish custom, the dead body was anointed with aromatic oils and salves and then wrapped in a long linen cloth. This had not been done before because Jesus had been buried in such a hurry in the tomb of Joseph of Arimathea. As soon as the law about resting on the Sabbath allowed, Mary Magdalene, Mary the mother of James, and Salome left their homes to go buy spices and oils to anoint Jesus' body.

Early the next morning they went to visit the tomb. As they were going on the road, they wondered who could roll the heavy stone away from the entrance to the sepulcher, so that they could get into where the body of Jesus lay? When they arrived at the tomb, they discovered that the stone already had been rolled away. With great fear they carefully made their way into the sepulcher. And in the place where the dead Jesus had been laid they saw an angel all dressed in white.

And he said to them, "Do not be amazed; you seek Jesus of Nazareth, who was crucified. He has risen, he is not here; see the place where they laid him. But go, tell his disciples and Peter that he is going before you to Galilee; there you will see him, as he told you."

(Mark 16:6-7)

This is how Mark told the story of the discovery of the empty tomb. John's account included other details that made the whole story much clearer. John told how Mary Magdalene ran to tell Peter, who was with John, what the women had discovered. Mary Magdalene cried out, "They have taken the Lord out of the tomb, and we do not know where they have laid him" (John 20:2).

Amazed, the two disciples ran to the tomb themselves. John, who was younger, ran faster than Peter and reached the tomb first. He, too, saw that the tomb had been opened. He looked in and saw on the ground the cloths in which Jesus had been wrapped; the cloth which had covered his head was rolled up beside them. However, John waited for Peter before actually entering. While waiting in front of the empty tomb, he understood. "He saw and believed" (John 20:8). Jesus was no longer among the dead.

55 That evening two disciples
were walking to Emmaus,
a village near Jerusalem.
A stranger joined them.
He stayed with them for supper.
As they ate together,
they realized that it was Jesus.

Luke added in his gospel other important details
about the risen Christ. The resurrection was not
simply the case of an empty tomb or a body found
to be missing. The risen Christ spoke with his
disciples, taught them, explained the Scriptures to
them, encouraged them, and even ate with them.
He was different from what he had been before;
he could vanish from their sight at any time.
Nevertheless his presence was real. Luke added
details about some of these encounters with Jesus.

Some hours after the empty tomb was discovered, two of Jesus' disciples were leaving Jerusalem. They were headed towards the village of
Emmaus, about six miles away. Perhaps they were
returning to their own homes, or perhaps they just
wanted to leave the city because of the sorrowful
events of the past few days.

Whatever the reason, they were on the road,
discussing the events of the past few days, when
a third traveler joined them. The stranger listened
to their conversation for a while and then asked
what they were talking about. This question amazed
the two disciples. Was it possible anyone around
Jerusalem had not heard about what had happened? People were talking of nothing else
throughout the entire city! One of the two disciples, whose name was Cleopas, tried to explain
to the stranger.

"Are you the only visitor to Jerusalem who
does not know the things that have happened
there in these days?" And he said to them,
"What things?" And they said to him, "Concerning Jesus of Nazareth, who was a prophet
mighty in deed and word before God and all
the people, and how our chief priests and rulers
delivered him up to be condemned to death,
and crucified him. But we had hoped that he
was the one to redeem Israel. Yes, and besides
all this, it is now the third day since this happened. Moreover, some women of our company amazed us. They were at the tomb early
in the morning and did not find his body; and
they came back saying that they had even seen
a vision of angels, who said that he was alive."
(Luke 24:18-23)

The disappointed disciple obviously had once placed great hope in Jesus. The response of the newcomer was surprising; he reproved the two disciples:

And he said to them, "O foolish men, and slow of heart to believe all that the prophets have spoken! Was it not necessary that the Christ should suffer these things and enter into his glory?" And beginning with Moses and all the prophets, he interpreted to them in all the scriptures the things concerning himself.

(Luke 24:25-27)

Now the disciples were amazed that the stranger knew so many things. At this point, they arrived at the village of Emmaus. The disciples invited the stranger to stay with them because the day was nearly over. The stranger accepted. All three travelers went to the house of the disciples, where a meal was prepared.

When they were seated at the table, the stranger took a loaf of bread, pronounced a blessing over it, broke it, and gave it to the disciples. Suddenly there was no longer any doubt that the stranger was Jesus himself. Then he vanished. In fact, the disciples no longer needed his visible presence because, by then, they had *faith* in him.

In spite of all that they had been through, in spite of the long journey on foot from Jerusalem, the two disciples were too excited to stay in Emmaus. They set out immediately to return to Jerusalem to tell of their encounter.

But the surprises of that day were not yet complete. When they arrived in Jerusalem, they found the disciples assembled together; they were about to describe their experiences on the road to Emmaus when they were told, "The Lord has risen indeed, and has appeared to Simon" (Luke 24:34). The two disciples then told what had happened to them and how they had recognized Jesus "in the breaking of the bread" (Luke 24:35).

Then, suddenly, Jesus himself appeared again in their midst. "Peace be with you!" he greeted them. But they were amazed and frightened; and they stood silent and still.

And he said to them, "Why are you troubled, and why do questionings rise in your hearts? See my hands and my feet, that it is I myself; handle me, and see; for a spirit has not flesh and bones as you see that I have."

(Luke 24:38-40)

So that they would have no doubt that he was really there, Jesus asked for something to eat. The disciples gave Jesus a piece of cooked fish, which he ate.

56

On another occasion,
when some disciples
were fishing,
Jesus helped them find
a large catch of fish.
Then the disciples
ate with Jesus.
Peter affirmed his love
for Jesus,
and Jesus affirmed Peter's place
of leadership in the Church.

During his lifetime Jesus laid the foundation for the Church, the community of his disciples. His risen presence among them marked the true beginnings of this community, a gathering of God's children around a head with whom they celebrated the Eucharist.

However, the Church did not enjoy for long the visible presence of the risen Christ. For this reason the Gospel of John was especially concerned about preserving for us those encounters with Jesus after his resurrection.

After the resurrection of Jesus, some of the apostles returned to Galilee. They were back at their old trade of fishing. One day the apostles Peter, James, John, Thomas, and Nathanael were on the shore of the Sea of Galilee. When evening fell, they put out onto the lake to fish, but in the course of the whole night they failed to catch any-

thing. Discouraged, they were returning to land when they saw in the uncertain light of dawn a stranger on shore who asked if they had any fish.

When they replied that they had caught no fish, the stranger told them to cast their net on the right side of the boat. More out of respect than out of conviction, they cast their net as directed, and to their great astonishment they could barely haul in all the fish in the net.

Jesus had performed a similar miracle near there at the very beginning of his ministry. John was the first to recall this, and he said to Peter, "It is the Lord!" (John 21:7). When Peter heard that it was Jesus, he plunged into the water with his usual reckless enthusiasm. The other apostles brought the boat in, dragging the heavy catch of fish.

On the shore, a cooking fire was burning, with fish and bread on it. Jesus told them to bring some of the fish they had just caught. When it was cooked, he invited them to eat. He took bread and gave it to them; he did the same with the fish.

This story reminded the apostles of the Eucharist. But it was also an intimate encounter among friends. From now on his disciples could always encounter Jesus in the Eucharist and renew his friendship there.

The next episode carried the same message. It was clear from recent events that the disciples could become discouraged. So Jesus gave to one of the disciples, Peter, the task of supporting and guiding the others. The three responses of love that Jesus required of Peter were to make up for the three times that Peter had denied Jesus after Jesus had been arrested. At the same time, these three answers marked a solemn covenant between Peter and Jesus. Only in his love for Jesus could Peter find the strength to carry out the task Jesus was giving him.

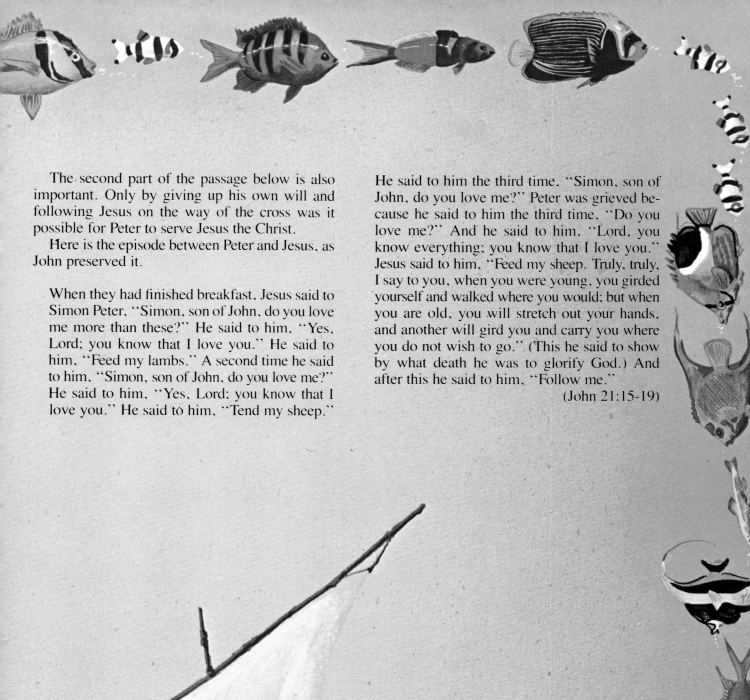

The second part of the passage below is also important. Only by giving up his own will and following Jesus on the way of the cross was it possible for Peter to serve Jesus the Christ.

Here is the episode between Peter and Jesus, as John preserved it.

When they had finished breakfast, Jesus said to Simon Peter, "Simon, son of John, do you love me more than these?" He said to him, "Yes, Lord; you know that I love you." He said to him, "Feed my lambs." A second time he said to him, "Simon, son of John, do you love me?" He said to him, "Yes, Lord; you know that I love you." He said to him, "Tend my sheep."

He said to him the third time, "Simon, son of John, do you love me?" Peter was grieved because he said to him the third time, "Do you love me?" And he said to him, "Lord, you know everything; you know that I love you." Jesus said to him, "Feed my sheep. Truly, truly, I say to you, when you were young, you girded yourself and walked where you would; but when you are old, you will stretch out your hands, and another will gird you and carry you where you do not wish to go." (This he said to show by what death he was to glorify God.) And after this he said to him, "Follow me."

(John 21:15-19)

57 Jesus gave his apostles the job of telling good news to the whole world and inviting all persons to be his disciples.

The apostles returned to Galilee after the death and resurrection of Jesus. Jesus had promised them that he would meet them there. The conclusion of the Gospel of Matthew contains the fulfillment of this promise and serves as a fitting conclusion of the entire gospel.

The eleven apostles assembled on a mountain in Galilee; there Jesus appeared to them. The detail that this meeting took place on a mountain is important. Moses delivered the Law to humanity from the top of a mountain. Matthew represented Jesus as a new Moses—in fact, someone superior to Moses—who proclaimed his new way of life, the Sermon on the Mount, from a mountain.

Jesus was the sign given to all nations; he was the Savior of all humankind. "All authority in heaven and on earth has been given to me," he said (Matthew 28:18). This truth about Jesus was the starting point for the mission on which Jesus sent the apostles. The world was a vast field. The apostles were given the task of sowing the seed in this vast field and of bringing in the harvest. In other words, they were given the task of preaching Jesus' message and baptizing those who ac-

cepted the message into membership in his body, the Church.

From the very beginning of Matthew's account, when he reported the coming of the magi from the east, the evangelist constantly emphasized the universal character of Jesus' mission and message to humanity. Now at the very end of his gospel, Matthew intended to make clear that everything written in his book, everything said

and done by Jesus, was of importance to every person in the world.

There remained, however, a great difference between pagan astrologers who came to seek Jesus and the apostles who were *sent out* to the whole world. In the end it is the Church, the community of Christians, that must take the initiative and go out to people, just as God took the initiative in sending Jesus to humanity. It was an enormous task, but the apostles would enjoy the constant presence and assistance of Jesus, who had again revealed himself as "Emmanuel," "God with us." The disciples became apostles by being sent out on his behalf.

The gospel passage with the last words of Jesus Christ to his apostles is the only place in all the four gospels where the Trinity—Father, Son, and Holy Spirit—is explicitly mentioned. According to some scholars, this invocation of the Trinity was a formula that the early Christians used in baptizing those who had been converted to faith in Jesus. Some think that it was added at the end of this gospel.

Now the eleven disciples went to Galilee, to the mountain to which Jesus had directed them. And when they saw him they worshiped him; but some doubted. And Jesus came and said to them, "All authority in heaven and on earth has been given to me. Go therefore and make disciples of all nations, baptizing them in the name of the Father and of the Son and of the Holy Spirit, teaching them to observe all that I have commanded you; and lo, I am with you always, to the close of the age."

(Matthew 28:16-20)

58 Jesus appeared for the last time
to his apostles
at his ascension.
Then he left them,
with the promise of the Spirit
and the mission to make disciples.

According to the evangelist Luke, the various appearances of Jesus to his disciples after his resurrection took place within a period of forty days. At the end of this period, Jesus appeared one final time, blessed his disciples, and then left the earth. The author used biblical images to picture the departure of Jesus. He ascended into the air and was taken up into the clouds which hid him from further view.

However, Jesus' dramatic departure from the earth in no way contradicted his promise that he would be with the apostles always. Rather, the end of his visible presence made way for a new kind of divine presence that would not end. With the coming of the Holy Spirit, the era of the Church would begin. The Spirit would make Jesus present to believers and would continually bring his teachings back to life in their hearts.

The ascension of Jesus helped prepare the apostles for Pentecost, the day when the Holy Spirit came. Once the Spirit had come, the apostles had no further need of the external, visible presence of Jesus because the Spirit brought Jesus into their hearts. So after the ascension of Jesus, the apostles returned with great joy to Jerusalem and began a life of regular praise and worship of God in the Temple.

There was another reason for the disciples' joy. When Jesus ascended, he entered into the new life of the kingdom where he had gone to prepare a place for his disciples.

Thinking about heaven should not distract Christians from the tasks that Jesus himself gave through the apostles, the mission to "make disciples of all nations." According to the Acts of the Apostles, the other New Testament book that Luke wrote, the disciples who kept gazing at the sky where they had last seen Jesus were reproved by two angels:

"Men of Galilee, why do you stand looking into heaven? This Jesus, who was taken up from you into heaven, will come in the same way as you saw him go into heaven." (Acts 1:11)

Once Jesus had been lost from sight, it was useless to go on gazing upwards. They had to go back to Jerusalem and get on with the task of teaching what Jesus had taught and of gathering into the Church of Christ those with ears to hear.

59 The gospels use many different names for Jesus.
All of them help us understand who he was.
The gospels also tell us about the Father and the Holy Spirit.

The Names of Jesus

Son of Man. This was what Jesus usually called himself. It is notable that this expression appears only in his own words. Neither the disciples nor the early Church used the name. In the Book of Daniel the prophet applies the term to the Messiah: " . . . with the clouds of heaven, there came one like a son of man" (Daniel 7:13). This meant that someone like a human being would come down from heaven, someone who was destined to have an eternal reign. Only Jews familiar with the Book of Daniel could understand the term; by using the title "Son of Man" for himself, Jesus was able to avoid using the term "Messiah," which his listeners might understand as meaning a political or military leader.

Messiah. The word actually means "consecrated by means of an anointing." It referred first to David the king. Then it was applied to a descendant of David's who was to come and rule over an eternal kingdom. Peter and then the other disciples recognized Jesus to be the promised Messiah. However, Jesus did not want this news spread around; he began teaching that the Messiah would be persecuted and put to death. He was trying to discourage the idea of an earthly, political, and nationalistic Messiah.

Christ. This word is the Greek translation of the Hebrew word *Messiah*, "anointed." In the Bible the name is usually used for Jesus only after his resurrection.

Son of David. This expression is the equivalent of "Messiah." According to the prophecies, the Messiah was to be a descendant of David, as Jesus was.

Rabbi. This is the Hebrew word for "teacher." In the Jewish religion, a rabbi was one who was learned in the Law. Rabbis taught people and usually had disciples who themselves often aspired to be rabbis or teachers in their turn. Jesus was called a teacher in this sense. But he taught on his own authority and did not merely repeat the traditional teaching.

Son of God. This title is found in the gospel of John and in the preaching and letters of Paul. Because Jesus is Son of God in a unique sense, Jesus can give human beings who believe in him "power to become children of God" (John 1:12).

Lord. This word corresponds to the Greek *Kyrios*, and in the Greek translations of the Old Tes-

Simon Peter

John

James

Andrew

Matthew

Philip

tament it was used for the name of God, *Yahweh*. After his resurrection, Jesus was commonly called "Lord" to indicate his authority and divinity.

The Twelve Apostles

The twelve apostles were chosen to work closest to Jesus, to preserve his teaching, to be witnesses to his resurrection, and, finally, to continue his mission; they were to go out to preach to the whole world. The number twelve is symbolic and has reference to the twelve tribes of Israel. The apostles were to be leaders of the new spiritual Israel, which is the Church.

The Disciples

The disciples were the people who regularly listened to Jesus and followed him. Of these disciples seventy-two were given certain preaching responsibilities. After the resurrection of Jesus, they and their families formed the nucleus of the Church, along with such women disciples as Mary Magdalene, Mary the wife of Clopas, Salome, and others. The number seventy-two is symbolic and refers to the traditional number of Gentile nations and of the peoples of the earth, according to the tables in Genesis 10.

Abba, Father

From Mark's account of Jesus' prayer in the garden of Gethsemane, we know that Jesus prayed to the Father using the Aramaic word *Abba*. This word is the everyday word for father; it is similar to "daddy" or "papa." Talking to God like this was something absolutely new. It gave the apos-

tles a better understanding of God's love. Like Jesus, the apostles themselves were authorized to call God "Abba." This was because they were united to God by faith. "Whoever loves me will obey my teaching. My Father will love him, and my Father and I will come to him and live with him" (John 14:23 TEV).

The Holy Spirit

This term was already in use in the Old Testament. There it meant a force coming from God that illuminated the prophets, guided the kings of Israel, and sometimes intervened to produce miraculous effects. Jesus made it clear that the Holy Spirit was more than a divine force. The Holy Spirit was a "person," just like the Father and the Son. The Spirit was revealed as the one who would make believers into the loving people God wanted them to be and as the guide and inspiration of the Church in leading persons to God and a fuller life. The Holy Spirit was also called by Jesus the Counselor or the Paraclete, that is, "Consoler, Comforter, Defender." Jesus promised the Holy Spirit to the apostles:

"I will pray the Father, and he will give you another Counselor, to be with you for ever, even the Spirit of truth, whom the world cannot receive, because it neither sees him nor knows him. . . . But the Counselor, the Holy Spirit, whom the Father will send in my name, he will teach you all things, and bring to your remembrance all that I have said to you."

(John 14:16-17,26)

Thaddeus	Thomas	James son of Alphaeus	Simon the Zealot	Bartholomew	Matthias

Outline by Chapter

JESUS
THE CHRIST

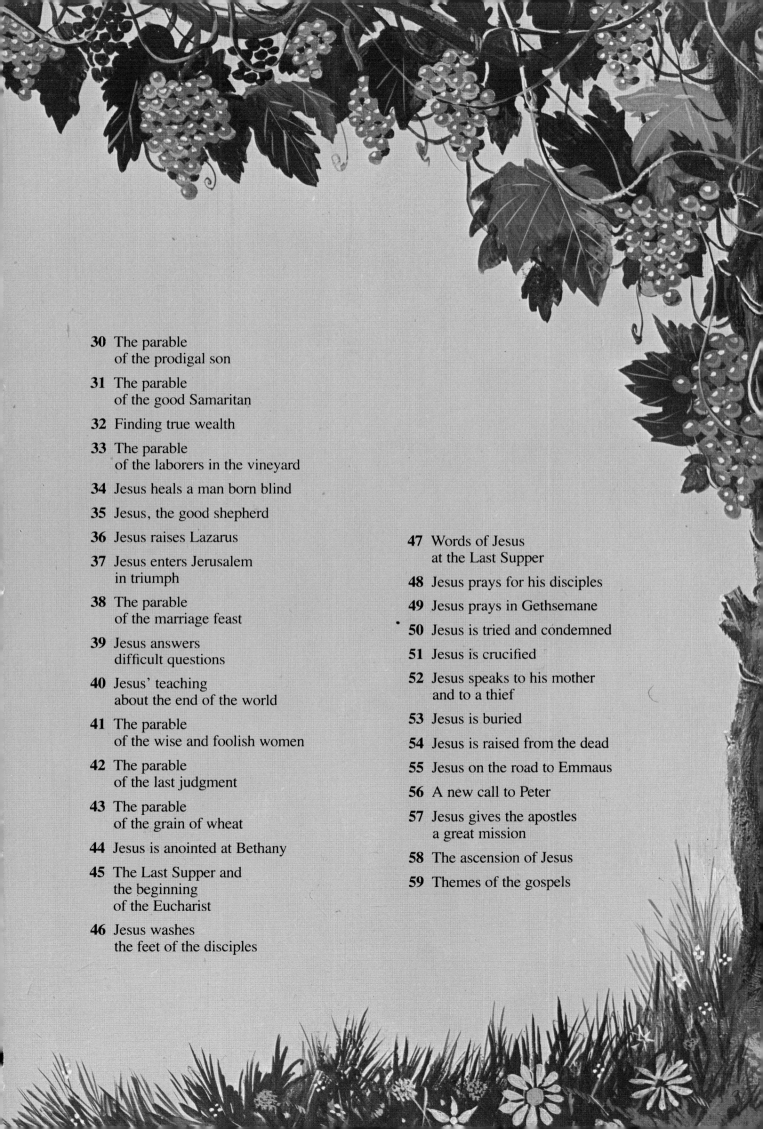